A LEADER'S GUIDE TO

What Young Children Need

to Succeed

Working Together to Build Assets from Birth to Age 11

Jolene L. Roehlkepartain
and Nancy Leffert, Ph.D.

free spirit
PUBLiSHiNG®

Works
for kids®

ISBN 1-57542-071-6

What Young Children Need to Succeed is based on *Starting Out Right: Developmental Assets for Children* by Nancy Leffert, Ph.D., Peter L. Benson, Ph.D., and Jolene L. Roehlkepartain, published in 1997 by Search Institute as part of Search Institute's national Healthy Communities • Healthy Youth Initiative, with support provided by Lutheran Brotherhood.

Cover design by Percolator
Illustrations by Marieka Heinlen
Book design and layout by Jessica Thoreson
Edited by Marjorie Lisovskis
Index prepared by Kay Schlembach

10 9 8 7 6 5 4 3 2 1
Printed in the United States of America

Free Spirit Publishing Inc.
400 First Avenue North, Suite 616
Minneapolis, MN 55401-1724
(612) 338-2068
help4kids@freespirit.com
www.freespirit.com

The following are registered trademarks of Free Spirit Publishing Inc.:

FREE SPIRIT®
FREE SPIRIT PUBLISHING®
SELF-HELP FOR TEENS®
SELF-HELP FOR KIDS®
WORKS FOR KIDS®
THE FREE SPIRITED CLASSROOM®

free spirit
PUBLiSHiNG®
Works for kids®

DEDICATION

To our families—
Gene, Micah, and Linnea Roehlkepartain
Mark, Jonathan, and Jeremy Leffert
and to all the adults who live with, teach, and care for young children.

ACKNOWLEDGMENTS

We thank Rebecca Grothe; Brenda Holben; Kay Hong; Irv Katz; Kathleen Kimball-Baker; Mary Nelson; Amy O'Leary; Gayle Olson; Barbara Pearce; Marilyn Peplau; Hilary Pert Stecklein, M.D.; Lesia Pikaart; Eugene Roehlkepartain; Amy Susman-Stillman, Ph.D.; Sandra Swanson; Terri Swanson; Nancy Tellett-Royce; Elanah Toporoff; and Cindy Wilcox for their careful review of earlier drafts of this book. We thank Amanda Seigel and Renee Vraa for their assistance in the preparation of this book. In addition, we are grateful to Amy Susman-Stillman, Ph.D., who helped to broaden and deepen how we have defined the developmental assets for children. Finally, we appreciate the thoughtful editorial work of Kathleen Kimball-Baker at Search Institute and Marjorie Lisovskis at Free Spirit Publishing.

Major support for Search Institute's work on developmental assets is provided by Lutheran Brotherhood, a not-for-profit organization providing financial services and community service opportunities for Lutherans worldwide. Additional support is provided by the Colorado Trust, Dewitt-Wallace Reader's Digest Fund, W.K. Kellogg Foundation, and others.

CONTENTS

LIST OF REPRODUCIBLE PAGES

INTRODUCTION

What do children need in order to grow up and succeed? Search Institute researchers have identified specific, practical things that can have a lasting positive impact on children. Rather than focus on problems, the researchers' work concentrates on *developmental assets*—positive things that all young people need. The assets are 40 building blocks that help children make wise decisions and choose positive lifestyles. Research on 6th to 12th graders has shown that the more of these assets young people experience, the better.

A Leader's Guide to What Young Children Need to Succeed includes five workshops that focus on building assets in infants, toddlers, preschoolers, and elementary-age children. This leader's guide is intended to be used with *What Young Children Need to Succeed* (the participants' book). Participants are asked to be familiar with portions of this book during each workshop, so you'll want to have several copies of it on hand. Ideally, each participant will have his or her own copy of the book.

ABOUT THIS BOOK

Both this leader's guide and the participants' book are based on research conducted by Search Institute. Since 1989, Search Institute researchers have surveyed young people in communities across the United States to learn what helps children grow up healthy, caring, and productive. Almost 100,000 young people in grades 6 through 12 have shared information about themselves and their lives since the surveys began.*

ORGANIZATION

This guide includes five workshops that address how to build assets in children from birth to age 11. Workshop 1: The Power of Children's Assets gives an overview and introduces the concept of children's assets. The remaining workshops present information about child development and practical ideas for building assets for children in the four specific age groups: infants (from birth to 12 months), toddlers (ages 13 to 35 months), preschoolers (ages 3 to 5 years), and elementary-age children (ages 6 to 11 years).

The purpose of the five workshops is to enhance people's understanding of children's assets as described in the participants' handbook, *What Young Children Need to Succeed*. Each workshop supports what people will read in the book and helps participants learn more about child development, the asset framework, and how to get started in building assets in young children.

---

*Both books are based in part on information from Search Institute's surveys of 99,462 6th–12th graders in 213 cities and towns across the United States during the 1996–1997 school year, the most current information available at the time of publication.

This guide also includes 50 handouts that give individuals a variety of practical suggestions for building developmental assets in children. The handouts are easy to read, understand, and use.

AUDIENCE

All five workshops can be easily adapted for many different audiences, including parents, childcare providers, educators, health-care professionals, congregational leaders, employers, librarians, and community leaders—in short, anyone who is interested in learning more about how to make a positive difference in children's lives.

The workshops have been tested across the country and have been successful with a diverse group of participants from a variety of cultural and socioeconomic backgrounds. They have been used with parents and guardians of single-parent families, blended families, two-parent families, and extended families who are raising children. In addition, the workshops have been used with teachers and other education professionals, classroom aides, childcare providers, recreation specialists, coaches, legislators, leaders of neighborhood organizations, community workers, children's club leaders, Scout leaders, music teachers, pediatricians and other health-care providers, religious educators and congregational program leaders for children, and child advocates. The participants' book offers a wealth of ideas for how nine different audiences can build assets in children: parents, childcare providers, educators, health-care professionals, congregational leaders, employers, librarians, community leaders, and children themselves. While suggestions appropriate to each audience are incorporated throughout the book, they are also addressed more specifically at the end of each asset group on pages 55–60, 82–87, 118–123, 147–153, 181–188, 222–227, 255–260, and 280–286.

You can conduct a workshop for as few as 5–10 people and as many as 100. These five workshops are designed for a workshop size of approximately 20–25 participants, but they can easily be adapted for groups of 100. You can also use the information to give a less interactive presentation to larger groups. You can tailor the ideas and sequence to best fit the audience you're working with.

GETTING READY TO CONDUCT WORKSHOPS

A Leader's Guide to What Young Children Need to Succeed is designed to help any individual introduce interested adults to Search Institute's framework of developmental assets for young children. There are no qualifications necessary to lead these workshops except a desire to support children, familiarity with developmental assets for children, and some experience in leading a group in a workshop format. By reading and studying the information presented in this leader's guide and in *What Young Children Need to Succeed*, you can equip yourself with the essential knowledge for conducting the workshops.

LINKING WITH ORGANIZATIONS

It's often easier to reach an audience when you're linked up with an organization or agency that can give you some support in holding a workshop or a series of workshops. There are many organizations willing and able to do this, including community education centers, preschools, Montessori schools, childcare centers, Head Start and Early Head Start programs, public and private elementary schools, religious institutions, family education programs, health-care centers, recreation programs, businesses, and children's organizations and clubs such as YMCA, YWCA, Girl Scouts, Boy Scouts, and Boys & Girls Clubs. See if there is an asset-building initiative in your community or school or in one of the organizations in your area. If you're already connected to an agency or organization, consider linking up with another group to reach a wider audience with the workshops.

STRUCTURING WORKSHOPS

There are as many ways to structure workshops on building assets in young children as there are leaders to plan and conduct them. Here are just a few ideas. Don't be limited by the suggestions that follow. For asset building to have the most impact, it needs to be presented in whatever format and time frame suits participants' needs.

Be creative. Be as creative as you like in structuring workshops. You might decide to present all or some of the workshops in a full-day or half-day session. You might run workshops once a week for two hours over five weeks, or for one hour over ten. Each workshop includes an overview telling the time to allow for individual activities. Use these guidelines to help you plan for the group and time you have.

Because the workshops are flexible, you may use the formats exactly as they're presented, or conduct them in different combinations. Workshops 2–5 have enough variety that they can be used as a series without undue repetition of content across the different age groups. Many of the activities can be tailored to other age groups, so become familiar with all of them and then add or adapt activities to provide more support for a specific age group or interest group.

Give individual seminars or speeches. You can customize your own training seminars or speeches by adapting the workshop activities. You might conduct Workshop 2: Building Assets in Infants at your local hospital in the maternity ward and then offer the Workshop 5: Building Assets in Elementary-Age Children at a local elementary school, perhaps sponsored by the PTA or PTO. If most of your participants are unfamiliar with children's assets, consider splitting the first workshop into two longer sessions so participants can more slowly digest the information and gain extra hands-on practice in building assets. If you have only an hour to present an overview in a speech format, use the text and reproducible handouts to highlight content you wish to present.

Offer family workshops. You can also create workshops where children and parents come together. For example, you might follow a 90-minute format. For the first hour, childcare providers or recreation leaders could spend time with children while the parents take part in the workshop. Then, for the last half-hour, you could bring parents and children together, using the time to teach families new, asset-building ways to interact with each other through games and other activities. A creative childcare provider, child-development expert, or recreation leader could teach age-appropriate games and activities for this purpose.

You might also create sibling classes so that older siblings can learn how to interact with a newborn or younger sibling. Or structure a class where kids explore ideas to build their own assets. For this purpose, you'll find reproducible "Ideas for Children" pages in *What Young Children Need to Succeed* at the end of each categorized asset section.*

OTHER IDEAS FOR PLANNING WORKSHOPS

Here are a few other ideas for conducting workshops:

- Offer a workshop twice: once during the day and once during the evening. This will allow you to reach parents, educators, childcare providers, and others whose schedules tie them up during either of those time periods.

- Offer a workshop during the lunch hour at various places of employment throughout your community. (Check with each business individually to arrange for this.) Interested adults could bring a sack lunch.

- Incorporate the workshops into conferences and community events. Have one large introductory workshop (using Workshop 1) and then have the other four workshops meet in separate areas at the same time. Participants can choose to attend the workshop that best fits the age group they work with and their own interests and needs.

- Create a half-day or full-day workshop for childcare providers, educators, or parents. Public and private schools are often looking for practical, new information that they can use for teacher training and development. A number of school districts have created asset-building teacher initiatives that have ignited a lot of interest within the schools and the community. You could also offer full- or half-day training to librarians, pediatricians, or a human services agency.

- Tap into the possibilities of religious institutions. Many offer adult learning hours and are looking for new topics to present.

- Monitor the knowledge depth of your audience. If participants are already familiar with the asset framework, feel free to use just one or two of the workshops or to pick and choose activities within each one. If you're introducing people to children's

---

*If your group includes preteens and teens, you'll find ideas for older kids in *What Kids Need to Succeed: Proven, Practical Ways to Raise Good Kids*, rev. ed., and *What Teens Need to Succeed: Proven, Practical Ways to Shape Your Own Future* by Peter L. Benson, Ph.D., Judy Galbraith, M.A., and Pamela Espeland (Minneapolis: Free Spirit Publishing, 1998).

assets for the first time, or if you have limited time and want to reach participants whose children are of different ages, Workshop 1 offers a broad overview.

- Offer childcare at no or low cost. This often boosts parent attendance. Make sure you have adequate staffing. One adult can't take care of 20 young children of different ages at the same time. The National Association for the Education of Young Children (NAEYC) says that one adult can care for 3–4 infants, 4–6 toddlers, or 7–10 preschoolers. The National School-Age Care Alliance says that one adult can care for 8–10 children between the ages of 5 and 6, and one adult can care for 10–15 children who are ages 6 to 11. If you offer childcare for children from birth to age 11, you'll need to set up different places for children: one area for infants and toddlers, another area for preschoolers, and another area for school-age children. To adequately staff childcare, have adults preregister their childcare needs, but also expect some children who aren't preregistered.

Your Workshop Goals

The workshops in this guide are meant to be a start. Use them "as is" or adapt the workshops to create new ones based on the particular needs of you and your group. Follow your instincts in developing what will work best in your particular setting. The three key things you want participants to learn are (1) the asset framework and how to build young children's assets, (2) what to expect of young children at each stage of development, and (3) the importance of building assets that fit children's age and abilities. What could be more fun—and educational?

LEADER PREPARATION

Follow these steps to prepare to lead asset-building workshops:

1. Read the participants' book and the leader's guide. Familiarize yourself with both the asset framework for all children and the ideas on how to build assets in infants, toddlers, preschoolers, and elementary-age children.

Read the introduction to the leader's guide and all of Workshop 1, which will provide additional information on 6th graders and assets. This information forms the basis for much of the asset framework.

Read through each of the other individual workshops before you lead it. You may want to make presentation notes on the pages of the guide that will help you as you conduct the workshop.

2. Plan the time. Decide how many workshops you plan to give and how long each workshop will last. Workshop 1 is designed to last 60–120 minutes. Workshops 2–5 are each designed to last 60–90 minutes. Each workshop includes an overview of the time required for each activity, so you can pare down, extend, or combine activities easily.

3. Schedule the workshops. Set the dates, times, and locations for all the workshops you'll be conducting. Then publicize the workshops to your potential audience.

4. Gather materials ahead of time. Depending on the budget—yours and your participants'—you'll want to arrange to have a copy of *What Young Children Need to Succeed* for each participant who attends your workshop. You may ask participants to purchase books ahead of time, sell the books at the workshop, loan books out for the duration of the workshops, or give participants free books that you or your organization has obtained.

Decide how you'll use the book in your workshop. Will you get it to participants before the workshop so they can read it as a prerequisite? Will you give it to participants at the beginning of the workshop and build in time for participants to read certain sections during the workshop? Will you distribute the book at the end of the workshop as a send-off for participants? (If you're presenting a series of workshops on children's assets that will be attended by the same people, you'll want to remind them to bring their copy of the participants' book to each workshop.)

If you have access to an overhead projector, you may want to make overheads of some of the reproducible handouts.

If participants register ahead of time, create a participant list to distribute. Often people want to connect with other people who share their interests and concerns. Creating a sense of community for adults is an important part of building young children's assets.

5. Prepare to answer participants' questions. Become familiar with resources on child development and age-appropriate activities. You'll find several of these in the "Helpful Resources" section, pages 13–15. The information you learn will help you answer questions, expand your group's discussion, and point participants to additional reading material.

It's particularly important to be ready to deal with people who express frustrations that show they're having difficulty coping. You'll want to have available the name and phone number of counselors, social workers, or other professionals in case participants want a referral or in case you want to suggest one. Don't hesitate to refer participants to professionals if you feel the issues being raised are beyond your comfort level and scope. Use discretion in doing this. It's usually best to approach an individual participant privately about this during a break, at the end of the workshop, or by phone soon after.

It's possible that you'll hear or observe a situation where a child is in need of protection. You have an obligation to follow through on this. Regulations governing the reporting of child abuse differ from state to state. Many states have specific guidelines identifying certain professionals as "mandatory reporters." Depending on the setting or settings that are involved in your workshops, check with the principal or agency head to determine the proper course of action and your responsibilities if such a situation should arise. Check on this before conducting workshops so you'll know what to do.

6. Prepare the room. Organize the room you'll be presenting in so that participants feel included and welcomed. For smaller groups (20 people or fewer), it's often a good idea to arrange the chairs in a circle. Plan to be a part of the circle or to conduct the workshop from the center. If you're using overheads, all the chairs will need to face in one direction so everyone can see. For interactive activities within each workshop, encourage participants to move their chairs to form small groups.

THE BASIC WORKSHOP FORMAT

The leader's guide provides you with clear and complete instructions for conducting the workshops. Each workshop is presented in a logically organized, step-by-step way. Much of the presentation material in the workshops is scripted (in boldface type) so you can literally read many parts aloud, if you like. Our goal was to create a guide that would be welcoming and easy to use for any group leader, beginning or experienced. The workshops are:

Workshop 1: The Power of Children's Assets
Workshop 2: Building Assets in Infants
Workshop 3: Building Assets in Toddlers
Workshop 4: Building Assets in Preschoolers
Workshop 5: Building Assets in Elementary-Age Children

Each workshop includes the following parts:

- **Workshop Overview:** Instructional goals for the workshop, an overview of the workshop activities with inclusive times, a list of specific readings and pages from the participants' book, a list of all handouts (with page numbers) for the workshop, and directions for what you need to do to prepare to lead the individual workshop

- **Activities:** 7 activities, each beginning with the teaching point(s), time, and materials needed; complete instructions for the activity including information, small-group and individual interactions, and key points to make

- **Other Options:** Ideas for extending or adapting the workshop activities

- **Looking Ahead:** A reminder to assign the reading for the next workshop

ABOUT DEVELOPMENTAL ASSETS FOR CHILDREN

What Young Children Need to Succeed makes the case that developmental assets are important for young children. Search Institute has surveyed young people across the country, and they have identified 40 key factors that make a powerful difference in young people's lives. This research showed that the *more* assets young people have, the *more* likely they are to become caring, competent, contributing adults, and the *less* likely they are to lose their way and get into trouble.

It's reasonable to infer that if assets are good for young people ages 12 and up, they're also good for younger children. Most child development experts agree that children need to start out right from day one. Data pertaining to 6th–12th graders is included here (some of it is also in Workshop 1) to give some insight into what young people at the end of the early childhood years and throughout middle school and high school report about themselves, their behavior, and their assets. This information can guide us as we seek to build assets in younger children.

Search Institute researchers found that the total number of assets makes a difference in young people's lives. These researchers have set the desired number of assets for each young person at 31 or more assets. Yet few 6th graders reported having that many assets. Only 15 percent of 6th graders reported having 31 to 40 assets.*

NUMBER OF ASSETS REPORTED BY 6TH GRADERS

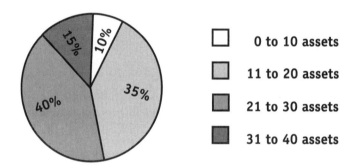

☐ 0 to 10 assets

◻ 11 to 20 assets

▨ 21 to 30 assets

■ 31 to 40 assets

In comparison, only 8 percent of the total sample (which includes 6th–12th graders) have 31 to 40 assets.

NUMBER OF ASSETS REPORTED BY 6TH–12TH GRADERS

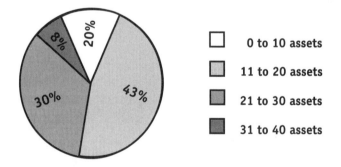

☐ 0 to 10 assets

◻ 11 to 20 assets

▨ 21 to 30 assets

■ 31 to 40 assets

*The statistics on pages 8–12 are based on surveys of 9,861 6th graders and 99,462 6th–12th graders in 213 cities and towns across the United States during the 1996–1997 school year, the most current information available at the time of publication.

If you look at the average number of assets that young people have, you'll see that 6th graders report the highest average of developmental assets (21.5 assets). The average number of assets drops every year until 12th grade, when the average number increases slightly.

NUMBER OF ASSETS REPORTED BY 6TH–12TH GRADERS

Grade 6	21.5
Grade 7	19.8
Grade 8	17.8
Grade 9	17.4
Grade 10	16.9
Grade 11	16.9
Grade 12	17.2
Total	18.0

How do we know the total number of assets is important? Search Institute researchers identified risk-taking behaviors (behaviors that potentially limit a young person's well-being) and found that reports of these risk-taking behaviors go down as the number of assets a young person reports goes up. Here are some examples of this among 6th graders:

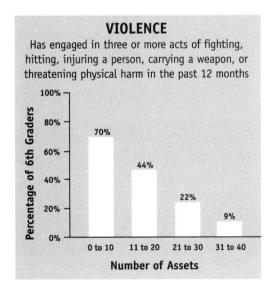

VIOLENCE
Has engaged in three or more acts of fighting, hitting, injuring a person, carrying a weapon, or threatening physical harm in the past 12 months

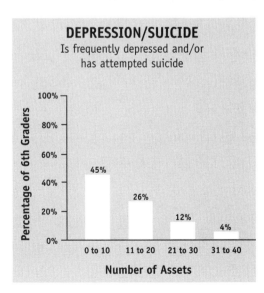

DEPRESSION/SUICIDE
Is frequently depressed and/or has attempted suicide

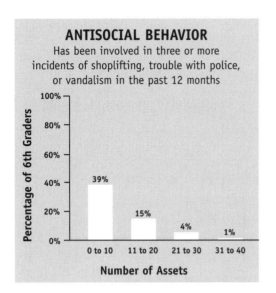

ANTISOCIAL BEHAVIOR

Has been involved in three or more incidents of shoplifting, trouble with police, or vandalism in the past 12 months

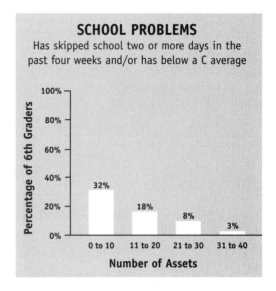

SCHOOL PROBLEMS

Has skipped school two or more days in the past four weeks and/or has below a C average

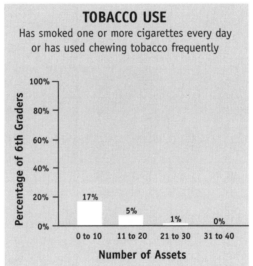

TOBACCO USE

Has smoked one or more cigarettes every day or has used chewing tobacco frequently

Researchers also found that the *more* assets a young person has, the more likely it is that the child will engage in positive behaviors—called *thriving indicators.* For all eight positive behaviors studied, young people who report more assets are more likely to act in these positive ways.

A Leader's Guide to What Young Children Need to Succeed

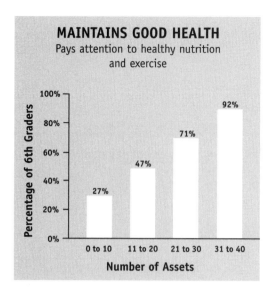

MAINTAINS GOOD HEALTH
Pays attention to healthy nutrition and exercise

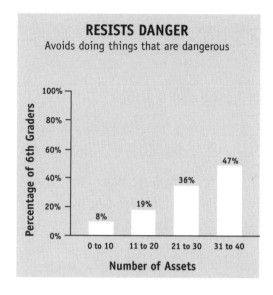

RESISTS DANGER
Avoids doing things that are dangerous

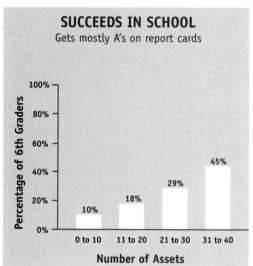

SUCCEEDS IN SCHOOL
Gets mostly A's on report cards

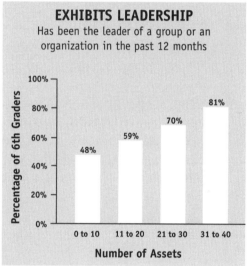

EXHIBITS LEADERSHIP
Has been the leader of a group or an organization in the past 12 months

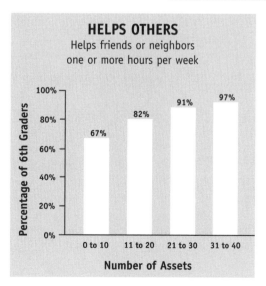

HELPS OTHERS
Helps friends or neighbors one or more hours per week

By looking at the data, Search Institute has identified that there is a clear percentage decline in levels of "child well-being" from 6th to 12th grade. This suggests that individual assets may decrease over the years.

ACTUAL LEVELS OF EACH ELEMENT OF CHILD WELL-BEING

	6th Graders	12th Graders
Number of Developmental Assets (Out of 40)	21.5	17.2
High-Risk Behavior Patterns (Out of 10)	1.2	3
Thriving Indicators (Out of 8)	4.5	4

The asset framework for children is a useful tool for educating parents, childcare providers, educators, and others who work with children. Through your workshops, you have an opportunity to help participants internalize a vision for healthy children, equipping them with the skills they need to build children's assets and motivating them with the message that the caring, support, and guidance they offer to children are critically important.

HELPFUL RESOURCES

 Here's a selection of books on developmental assets and on Search Institute's data about 6th graders, resources on child development, and books on spending time with children in enjoyable ways. Use these recommended readings as a starting point. Also see pages 296–304 in *What Young Children Need to Succeed* for other helpful resources on child development and asset building.

ASSETS AND THE 6TH-GRADE DATA

The Fragile Foundation, by Peter L. Benson, Peter C. Scales, Nancy Leffert, and Eugene C. Roehlkepartain (Minneapolis: Search Institute, 1999). The most current report available on the data of 6th–12th graders and developmental assets, this book includes a wide range of statistics about young people's well-being. You'll find detailed analysis of the developmental assets, risky behaviors, deficits, and thriving indicators.

CHILD DEVELOPMENT

INFANTS (BIRTH TO 12 MONTHS)

The New First Three Years of Life: New and Revised Edition by Burton L. White (New York: Fireside, 1995). This classic book is a detailed guide of the mental, physical, social, and emotional development of infants and toddlers. The new and revised edition is full of practical ideas on how to discipline effectively, which toys to give young children, and how to defuse sibling rivalry.

What to Expect the First Year by Arlene Eisenberg, Heidi E. Murkoff, and Sandee E. Hathaway, B.S.N. (New York: Workman Publishing, 1989). A comprehensive month-by-month guide explains what parents can expect (and how to respond) as babies develop.

TODDLERS (AGES 13 TO 35 MONTHS)

Your One-Year-Old: Fun-Loving and Fussy by Louise Bates Ames, Ph.D.; Frances L. Ilg, M.D.; and Carol Chase Haber, M.A. (New York: Dell, 1982). Focusing on the issues confronting 12- to 24-month-old children, the authors examine the various stages of development between infancy and toddlerhood. The authors have also written: *Your Two-Year-Old: Terrible or Tender* (New York: Dell, 1976), which offers insights into how 2-year-olds behave with family members and other children—and how to respond.

What to Expect: The Toddler Years by Arlene Eisenberg, Heidi E. Murkoff, and Sandee E. Hathaway, B.S.N. (New York: Workman Publishing, 1994). This guide gives information on what to expect from 13 months to 36 months. It also includes an extensive section on toddler care, health, and safety.

PRESCHOOLERS (AGES 3 TO 5 YEARS)

Your Three-Year-Old: Friend or Enemy by Louise Bates Ames, Ph.D., and Frances L. Ilg, M.D. (New York: Dell, 1985). The authors point out that emotional insecurity is often at the heart of a 3-year-old's personality and suggest ways to deal with fears, toilet training, eating habits, and developing language skills. The authors have also written *Your Four-Year-Old: Wild and Wonderful* (New York: Dell, 1976) and *Your Five-Year-Old: Sunny and Serene* (New York: Dell, 1979).

Caring for Your Baby and Young Child: Birth to Age 5 by the American Academy of Pediatrics (New York: Bantam, 1993). This book gives detailed information, with chapters focusing on specific ages. In addition to health issues, the authors discuss family issues, childcare, and dealing with behavior.

ELEMENTARY-AGE CHILDREN (AGES 6 TO 11 YEARS)

Your Six-Year-Old: Loving and Defiant by Louise Bates Ames, Ph.D., and Frances L. Ilg, M.D. (New York: Dell, 1979). This book explores how the relationship between the child and the mother changes during this year and how mothers can deal with the changes. The authors have also written *Your Seven-Year-Old: Life in a Minor Key* (New York: Dell, 1976), *Your Eight-Year-Old: Lively and Outgoing* (New York: Dell, 1989), *Your Nine-Year-Old: Thoughtful and Mysterious* (New York: Dell, 1990), and *Your Ten- to Fourteen-Year-Old* (New York: Dell, 1988).

Caring for Your School-Age Child: Ages 5 to 12 by the American Academy of Pediatrics (New York: Bantam, 1995). This comprehensive book details what's normal and what's not, pointing out the importance of these formative years.

TOGETHER TIME

FOR ADULTS AND INFANTS (BIRTH TO 12 MONTHS)

Games to Play with Babies by Jackie Silberg (Mt. Rainier, MD: Gryphon House, 1993). This book includes 250 fun-filled games for caregivers and parents to play with babies.

No Bored Babies by Jan Fisher Shea (Seattle: Bear Creek, 1991). Find creative ideas on how to play with infants in ways that stimulate their development.

For Adults and Toddlers (Ages 13 to 35 Months)

Things to Do with Toddlers and Twos and *More Things to Do with Toddlers and Twos* by Karen Miller (West Palm Beach: Telshare, 1984). Each of these books is packed with 400 activities that help adults stimulate toddlers' language development and sensory exploration.

Games to Play with Toddlers (Mt. Rainier, MD: Gryphon House, 1993) and *More Games to Play with Toddlers* (Mt. Rainier, MD: Gryphon House, 1996) by Jackie Silberg. These two books present creative games that encourage toddlers' natural curiosity and desire to explore their environment.

For Adults and Preschoolers (Ages 3 to 5 Years)

Fidget Busters (Loveland, CO: Group Books, 1992) and *Wiggle Tamers* (Loveland, CO: Group Books, 1995) by Jolene L. Roehlkepartain. These two books highlight 25 games to play with preschoolers and 25 games to play with groups of preschoolers and elementary-age children together.

500 Five-Minute Games: Quick and Easy Activities for 3- to 6-Year-Olds (Mt. Rainier, MD: Gryphon House, 1995) and *300 Three-Minute Games: Quick and Easy Activities for 2- to 5-Year-Olds* (Mt. Rainier, MD: Gryphon House, 1997) by Jackie Silberg. From imagination games to stuffed animal games, these two books are full of creative, fun ways that adults and preschoolers can play together.

For Adults and Elementary-Age Children (Ages 6 to 11 Years)

The New Games Book (New York: Dolphin, Doubleday, 1976) and *More New Games!* (New York: Dolphin, Doubleday, 1981) by Andrew Fluegelman. These classic game books present creative ways for adults and children to have fun together.

Fidget Busters (Loveland, CO: Group Books, 1992) and *Wiggle Tamers* (Loveland, CO: Group Books, 1995) by Jolene L. Roehlkepartain. These two books highlight 25 games to play with kids in kindergarten to 3rd grade, 25 games to play with 4th to 6th graders, and 25 games to play with groups of different-aged children.

THE WORKSHOPS

Workshop 1

THE POWER OF CHILDREN'S ASSETS

PARTICIPANTS WILL

- gain a basic understanding of the developmental asset framework for children.
- understand some of the fundamental issues in child development and how they relate to asset building.
- identify some specific ways they can begin to build assets in children.

TIME

Activity	Time
1. Introducing Developmental Assets for Children	10–30 minutes
2. Your Asset-Building Journey	10–15 minutes
3. The Children Around Us	15–20 minutes
4. The Assets for Children	10–15 minutes
5. The ABCs and XYZs of Building Young Children's Assets	5–10 minutes
6. Getting Practical	5–10 minutes
7. Daily Acts of Asset Building	5–10 minutes
Total	**60–120 minutes**

RELATED SECTIONS IN *WHAT YOUNG CHILDREN NEED TO SUCCEED*

- Introduction, pages 1–7
- The Power of Developmental Assets, pages 8–12
- The Assets Defined, pages 13–23
- Making Asset Building Part of Your Everyday Life, pages 287–295

REPRODUCIBLE HANDOUTS USED IN WORKSHOP 1

Have ready a copy of each of the following reproducible handouts for each participant:

PREPARATION

Before leading this workshop, complete handout #35: Your Asset-Building Journey. This will help you prepare for conducting Activity 2.

Optional: Create a ball out of about 50–100 rubber bands to use in Activity 7.

ACTIVITIES

1. INTRODUCING DEVELOPMENTAL ASSETS FOR CHILDREN

TEACHING POINT   Building assets is a positive way to ensure that children grow up healthy.

MATERIALS
- *What Young Children Need to Succeed,* pages 1–3 and 8–12
- Handout #1: 40 Developmental Assets for 6th Graders
- Handout #2: The Power of Developmental Assets
- Handout #3: The Power of Assets to Protect 6th Graders
- Handout #4: 6th Graders Acting in Positive Ways

Note: If participants aren't familiar with developmental assets, allow 30 minutes for this activity so group members will have enough time to learn the information presented.

*Allow **10–30 minutes** for this activity*

Introduce the concept of developmental assets to the group. You might say: **Since 1989, Search Institute researchers have been surveying young people in communities across the United States to learn what helps children grow up healthy, caring, and productive. As a result of this research, Search has identified 40 key factors that make a powerful difference in young people's lives. These factors are called** *developmental assets.* **They include things like family support, a caring neighborhood, self-esteem, and positive values.**

The Search surveys have been conducted with young people in grades 6 through 12. It's reasonable to infer that if assets are good for older children, they're also good for younger children. A healthy beginning can help children develop their full potential. Caring adults can build assets in even the youngest child.

Use the handouts to present the 40 assets and explain what research has shown about developmental assets in 6th graders:

Distribute Handout #1. Say: **This handout presents the 40 developmental assets 6th-grade children need to succeed. It shows the percentages of children surveyed who reported having each developmental asset in their lives.**

Although each of the 40 assets is important for each child, you'll notice that 6th graders are apt to have more of some assets than others. The three assets 6th-grade children are *most* **likely to have are Asset 1: Family Support, Asset 15: Positive Peer Influence, and Asset 29: Honesty. The four assets 6th-grade children are** *least* **likely to have are Asset 7: Community Values Youth, Asset 17: Creative Activities, Asset 25: Reading for Pleasure, and Asset 32: Planning and Decision Making.**

Distribute Handout #2. Say: **The developmental assets are powerful. By surveying nearly 100,000 kids in grades 6 through 12, Search Institute learned just how powerful they are. For example, the more assets a young person has, the less likely that child is to get involved in risky behaviors. The top two charts on the handout show how 2 types of risky behaviors go down as assets go up. Search Institute's researchers have consistently found positive connections between the assets and 24 risky behaviors.**

It's also true that the more assets young people have, the more likely they are to grow up doing positive things. The bottom two charts on the handout show how 2 types of positive behavior go up as assets go up. Search Institute's researchers found positive connections between the assets and 8 positive behaviors.

Distribute Handout #3. Say: **This handout shows the percentages of 6th graders surveyed who reported engaging in 24 risky and dangerous behaviors. The top 5 risky behaviors reported for 6th graders are hitting, riding with someone who's under the influence of alcohol, gambling, threatening to physically harm someone, and participating in group fighting.**

Distribute Handout #4. Say: **This handout shows the percentages of 6th graders surveyed who reported engaging in 8 positive behaviors. The top 2 positive behaviors reported for 6th graders are helping others and overcoming adversity—not giving up when things get difficult.**

Talk about how the assets protect children and promote positive behavior. Also talk about the implications of the 6th-grade data and what it suggests for younger children. Point out that it makes sense to conclude that building assets in younger children will help support the children as they grow.

KEY POINTS TO MAKE

- Assets are 40 key building blocks that help children succeed.

- All children need assets.

- The more assets young people have, the *more* likely it is that they'll do positive things, such as succeed in school and exhibit leadership skills.

- The more assets young people have, the *less* likely it is that they'll engage in risky behaviors, such as drinking alcohol, using other drugs, smoking, and acting in violent ways.

- We need to take seriously the risky behaviors of young children. For example, hitting and verbal threats need to be dealt with immediately so children clearly understand that these behaviors are inappropriate and dangerous. We also need to intervene when children act depressed, especially if sadness occurs often. Adults need to seek professional help for a depressed child.

- Younger children tend to have more assets than older teenagers; individual assets may decrease over the years. (See "About Developmental Assets for Children," pages 7–12, for more information about this point.)

2. Your Asset-Building Journey

TEACHING POINT

Each person has had a different experience growing up, but everyone can remember someone who touched her or his life and influenced it in a positive way.

MATERIALS

- Handout #35: Your Asset-Building Journey

*Allow **10–15** minutes for this activity*

Say: **No matter where we grew up or what kind of family we were in, as children nearly all of us experienced developmental assets. Some of us have had more asset-building experiences than others, but for this exercise, let's focus on the *types* of experiences we've had rather than the *number*.**

Referring to the copy of Handout #35 that you completed ahead of time, share with the group an asset-building activity you experienced as a child (for example, taking piano lessons). Also give examples of an asset-building relationship (for example, with your grandmother) and an asset-building place (the basketball court at your neighborhood park).

Distribute the handout to each person and allow about 5 minutes for participants to complete it. Afterward, ask for volunteers to share what they wrote.

KEY POINTS TO MAKE

- Most adults have probably had asset-building experiences as children, though they may not have identified the experiences as assets at that time.

- One of the key components of asset building is relationships. Most group members can probably name at least one adult who had a significant impact on them when they were children.

- Although the developmental asset framework focuses on children and youth, everyone needs assets. Adults as well as children need caring, supportive people around them. They need to spend their time doing constructive, meaningful things. Learning is still essential. Asset building is a life-long process.

- While it's more difficult to build assets in children when an adult doesn't have a strong personal base of assets, there are specific things nearly anyone can do that can help build personal assets. For example, to have more supportive adults in one's life (Asset 3), a person can join a band or choir, support group, sport team, or some other activity where it's possible to meet others who share the same interests. To boost a commitment to learning (Assets 21–25), an adult can take a community education class or read in-depth about a topic of interest. No matter what kind of childhood someone had, the person can still nurture his or her own personal assets.

3. THE CHILDREN AROUND US

TEACHING POINT

Many people and institutions in a community touch children's lives. All can help build assets.

MATERIALS

- 3 large sheets of paper (such as parcel paper or pages from a flip chart)
- 3 black thick-point markers
- 24 other markers in assorted colors (3 packs of 8 markers each)
- Masking tape

Allow **15–20 minutes** for this activity

Have participants form three groups. Give each group one large sheet of paper, one black thick-point marker, and an assortment of eight other markers. Assign each group one of these letters:

Y—representing the youngest children (infants and toddlers from birth to 35 months old)
E—representing early childhood (preschoolers ages 3 to 5 years)
S—representing school-agers (elementary-age children ages 6 to 11 years)

Have each group outline the designated letter in black marker on the piece of paper so that there's room on the inside of the letter to write words. Then have groups identify all the places and people who come into contact with that age group. For example, the Y group (infants and toddlers) may include on their letter a childcare center, a caregiver, and a sibling. The E group (preschoolers) may include a preschool, a parent-child swimming class, and a neighbor. The S group (school-age children) may include scouting, soccer, and school. Encourage groups to write as many different individuals, organizations, and institutions as they can think of. Have them write the words inside the outlined letter, using different-colored markers.

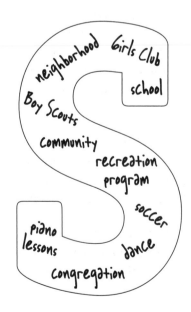

Have the Y group report to the larger group first. Tape the Y up on the wall. Have the E group report second; tape the E to the right of the Y. After the S group makes it report, hang up the S to the right of the E. Say: **These are all individuals, organizations, and institutions who can say "YES" to children. That's an important message children need to hear, and asset building can help us give children that message on a daily basis.**

4. THE ASSETS FOR CHILDREN

TEACHING POINT

Children need assets from the day they are born, but the specific assets vary a bit as children grow and change.

MATERIALS

- *What Young Children Need to Succeed,* pages 3–5 and 13–23
- Handout #5: 40 Assets Infants Need to Succeed
- Handout #6: 40 Assets Toddlers Need to Succeed
- Handout #7: 40 Assets Preschoolers Need to Succeed
- Handout #8: 40 Assets Elementary-Age Children Need to Succeed
- Handout #9: 40 Assets Middle and High School Kids Need to Succeed
- Handout #10: 40 Assets for Children and Teens

Allow **10–15 minutes** for this activity

Say: **All children need assets, and Search Institute has developed five lists of assets that can capture the specific needs of children at each stage of development.**

Distribute Handout #5. Say: **This is the list of 40 assets infants need to succeed. The language of the asset definitions focuses on how infants grow and change during the first year of life. Since parents and caregivers make many of the decisions for infants, you'll notice that many of the definitions address the central role of parents and caregivers in infants' lives.**

Distribute Handout #6. Say: **This is the list of 40 assets toddlers need to succeed. The language of the asset definitions for toddlers is different because of developmental differences between toddlers and infants. For example, while infants observe their world, toddlers tackle it. While infants stay in relatively close quarters, toddlers take off and explore. Like infants, toddlers interact with caregivers, but they're also busy exploring and getting into things.**

Distribute Handout #7. Say: **This is the list of 40 assets preschoolers need to succeed. The definitions reflect that preschoolers are starting to take a more active role in the world. Children between the ages of 3 and 5 are learning that their actions affect other people, and their rapidly growing language skills help them develop in new ways.**

Distribute Handout #8. Say: **This is the list of 40 assets elementary-age children need to succeed. The definitions reflect the fact that children 6 to 11 years old spend less time at home and more time at school and in other settings. People outside the family have a** greater influence in their lives. As their verbal and reasoning abilities expand, elementary-age children begin to think and act in ways that build their own assets.

Distribute Handout #9. Say: **This is the list of 40 assets for adolescents. Although our focus is on young children, it's equally important for all of us to build assets in older children as well.**

Distribute Handout #10. Say: **This is an overview of the 40 assets for children and adolescents. Here you'll see only the names of the assets, not the specific definitions. The handout shows the big picture of the developmental progression for building children's assets from birth to age 18.**

KEY POINTS TO MAKE

- Assets are built from the first day of a child's life, and we need to keep building these assets every day throughout a child's life.

- Although many of the asset names may be the same, the definitions reflect the developmental differences among these age groups. Participants should pay close attention to the definitions, particularly as they apply to the ages of children group members work with.

- The way to build assets depends on children's age. Building assets in an infant is different from building them in a preschooler; building assets in a 2-year-old is different from building them in an 8-year-old. (Page 4 in *What Young Children Need to Succeed* describes developmental differences in infants, toddlers, preschoolers, and elementary-age children.)

5. THE ABCS AND XYZS OF BUILDING YOUNG CHILDREN'S ASSETS

TEACHING POINT

Asset building can be easy.

MATERIALS

- Handout #36: The ABCs and XYZs of Building Young Children's Assets
- *What Young Children Need to Succeed*, pages 287–295

Allow **5–10 minutes** for this activity

Say: **Building assets doesn't need to be difficult or time-consuming. In fact, asset building can be as simple or as complex as you'd like. It can use a little of your time, or a lot. Many people prefer to start small. What's important is that you start to build assets for the children in your life.**

Distribute Handout #36 and go over the ideas with the group. Also relate some of the examples from *What Young Children Need to Succeed*, pages 289–295, that show simple ways individuals, organizations, and communities have built assets. Invite anecdotes or suggestions from group members as well.

6. GETTING PRACTICAL

TEACHING POINT

There are simple, specific things participants can do to start building assets right now.

MATERIALS

- Handout #37: Easy Ideas for Building Assets in All Young Children: A Worksheet

*Allow **5–10** minutes for this activity*

Have participants form groups with three or four people who are sitting near them. Explain the activity by saying: **One at a time, you'll give your name, tell where you're from, and talk about some ways you've already started to build assets—or could begin to build them—in young children you know.**

To help groups get started, give examples from your own life (such as learning the names of children in your neighborhood; volunteering an hour a month at a school, childcare center, or library; looking at ways to use the asset framework as a guide for setting policies at your workplace; posting a list of the 40 developmental assets on your refrigerator as a daily reminder).

Say: **In each group, the first person to talk will be the one who woke up the earliest this morning.** Then go around the circle to the right. Groups will have 5 minutes for this activity.

Bring all participants back together and invite volunteers to share some of the ideas they came up with. Distribute Handout #37 and encourage group members to record some ideas from the group activity. Also ask them to write down one easy idea for each age group that they can use right away to begin building young children's assets.

KEY POINTS TO MAKE

- Asset building can be simple. Just choose one thing and start there. For example, learning children's names is an important way to build assets.

- Asset building doesn't have to take a lot of your time. Even if your schedule is packed, you can find time to squat down and say hello to a toddler or smile at an 11-year-old.

- Let asset building tap into who you are. Do you like sports? Talk baseball or play T-ball with children. Are you interested in art? Do some finger painting with a child. Do you enjoy writing letters? Find out children's birthdays and send them a card every year. Do you like to bake? Make cookies with a child.

7. DAILY ACTS OF ASSET BUILDING

TEACHING POINT

It's important to stick with asset building. The little things done for children can really add up.

- *What Young Children Need to Succeed,* pages 6–7
- 2 rubber bands for each participant
- Handout #38: Facts About Young Children and Assets
- **Optional:** Ball you've created out of about 50–100 rubber bands

Allow **5–10 minutes** for this activity

Give each participant two rubber bands. Demonstrate how you scrunch up one rubber band and wrap the other around it to make an oddly shaped ball. Ask participants to do the same with their rubber bands. Say: **From now on, whenever you see a rubber band lying around, pick it up and stick it in your pocket. Bring it home and add it to your ball. Let each rubber band symbolize an act of asset building. A couple of rubber bands give the ball a start in taking shape; adding more and more rubber bands makes the ball larger and larger. In the same way, one or two acts of asset building can make a difference for a child, but many more acts have a far greater effect over time. Imagine how your rubber ball would look with fifty, a hundred, or a thousand rubber bands.** (If you have a sample ball, show it to the group.) **And if you were to do fifty, a hundred, or a thousand things to build children's assets, imagine how strong their asset base could be.**

Building assets can be easy. The important thing is to *start* **building assets and to make a commitment to** *continue* **doing it. Don't think of building assets as one of many chores to check off your to-do list. Instead, challenge yourself to build assets as often and in as many ways as you can. Children need these experiences and relationships every day throughout the years of childhood and adolescence. They need each of us to become a committed asset builder. So start now. Choose to be an asset builder every day in at least one simple way.**

Distribute Handout #38 to participants to take home and read on their own.

OTHER OPTIONS

As time permits and/or if participants are interested, distribute and discuss the information on Handouts #39 and #40. Invite group members to comment on the tips and to offer additional ideas for building assets in children who are gifted or have other special needs.

LOOKING AHEAD

At the end of the workshop, tell participants the time and place for the next workshop. Ask them to read some or all of the asset-building tips in *What Young Children Need to Succeed.* You may want to suggest that they focus on tips for the ages of the children they interact with. Suggest that they wear loose comfortable clothes for subsequent workshops, since they'll be asked to sit on the floor for some of the group activities.

Workshop 2

BUILDING ASSETS IN INFANTS

PARTICIPANTS WILL

- gain a basic understanding of the developmental assets for infants (birth to 12 months).
- examine some of the characteristics of typical development in infancy.
- identify some specific ways they can begin to build assets in infants.

TIME

Activity	Time
1. Understanding Infants	10–15 minutes
2. Introducing Developmental Assets for Infants	10 minutes
3. Asset Builders Supporting Adults	10 minutes
4. Floor Play with Infants	10–15 minutes
5. Building Assets in Infants	5–15 minutes
6. The Infant's World	10–15 minutes
7. First Steps	5–10 minutes
Total	**60–90 minutes**

RELATED SECTIONS IN *WHAT YOUNG CHILDREN NEED TO SUCCEED*

- About the Language Used in This Book, pages 3–5
- 40 Assets Infants Need to Succeed, pages 16–17
- Building the Assets, pages 25–286: all material under the headings "All Children" and "Infants"

REPRODUCIBLE HANDOUTS USED IN WORKSHOP 2

Have ready a copy of each of the following reproducible handouts for each participant:

PREPARATION

Before leading this workshop, familiarize yourself thoroughly with the information on Handouts #11, #12, and #13. You will need to know this material to conduct many of the activities.

ACTIVITIES

1. UNDERSTANDING INFANTS

TEACHING POINT
Infants communicate their needs nonverbally.

MATERIALS
- Flip chart (or 2 large sheets of paper)
- Marker
- Handout #11: What to Expect of Infants
- Handout #12: Tips for Talking with Infants

Allow 10–15 minutes for this activity

As a group, brainstorm a list of what infants communicate through their cries. Write these ideas on the flip chart or a large sheet of paper. (Examples will probably include hunger, wet diaper, fatigue, boredom, wanting to be held, and being overstimulated.) Read the list aloud when the group is finished.

Say: **Babies communicate from the moment they're born, but it isn't always clear what they're saying. Let's do an exercise on nonverbal communication to experience what it's like to communicate without words.**

Ask for a volunteer. Whisper in the volunteer's ear that he or she is to choose one of the following to communicate nonverbally to the group: the title of a movie about babies (such as *Three Men and a Baby, Baby Boom, Raising Arizona,* or *Look Who's Talking*) or a well-known baby's picture book (such as *Pat the Bunny, On the Day You Were Born, Good Night Moon,* or a Mother Goose book). Make it clear the volunteer is not to let other participants know that the chosen thing is a movie or a book.

Tell the group: **We're going to play a game of nonverbal charades. Our volunteer wants to communicate something to you, but you need to ask questions and try to guess what that is. The volunteer can use hand, face, and body movements and facial expressions. However, our volunteer cannot speak.**

When the exercise is over, ask the group:

- **Was it harder at first to understand what the volunteer was communicating? What helped you begin to understand?**

- **Can you imagine what it would be like to always communicate without words?**

- **What are some of the different ways infants tell us what they need from us?**

Brainstorm as a group. Write the ideas on a flip chart or large sheet of paper. Encourage participants to think of as many ways as possible. Suggestions might include waving arms, kicking feet, opening or closing the mouth or eyes, laughing, and so on.

Participants may wonder whether and why it's important to always respond to infants' needs immediately. Explain that infants cry less frequently and for shorter amounts of time when parents and caregivers respond to their cries immediately. Babies also learn that they can count on their parents and caregivers when these adults respond immediately in predictable, sensitive ways.

Next, distribute Handouts #11 and #12. Summarize and discuss the ideas on the handouts. Encourage participants to give examples from their own observations of how infants move, interact, learn, and talk and how adults can communicate positively with them.

KEY POINTS TO MAKE

- There is a rich form of communication that occurs between a baby and another individual. Even though the baby doesn't speak with words, a lot is communicated through gestures, body language, facial expressions, different cries, and vocal sounds. Although infants do not understand the words, the sound and intonation of the parent's or caregiver's voice are soothing and stimulating.

- It takes a while to learn how to understand a particular infant's language. Each infant communicates needs differently. As with the charade activity the group did, it may seem at first that the adult and infant will never understand each other. Yet, after awhile, communication gets easier. A helpful analogy is to think about a professional mime or charade player. In reality, the "professional" simply has more experience.

- As adults, we need to keep trying to understand. People sometimes joke about having a checklist of baby needs (point to the list the group brainstormed earlier). Although we joke about that, we seriously need to consider all the different messages an infant may be trying to give us.

- Sometimes it's difficult to decipher what a baby is communicating. Don't be hard on yourself if you're having trouble understanding. Keep trying to figure out what the baby wants to communicate, and keep showing your concern and support by being available. (Don't hesitate to ask other adults for their ideas, too.) Even if you don't always figure out the infant's specific need, your caring voice and attention will reassure the baby.

2. INTRODUCING DEVELOPMENTAL ASSETS FOR INFANTS

TEACHING POINT

The 40 assets help us understand and nurture the growth of infants.

MATERIALS

- Handout #5: 40 Assets Infants Need to Succeed
- *What Young Children Need to Succeed*, pages 3–5, 16–17, and 25–286

Allow **10 minutes** for this activity

Distribute Handout #5 and introduce the developmental asset framework for infants to participants. Point out the eight asset groups and some of the specific assets and asset definitions for infants. Emphasize the key roles parents, families, and other primary caregivers play in infants' lives. Also point out that there is a copy of the asset framework for infants on pages 16–17 of *What Young Children Need to Succeed*.

Briefly scan that book, pointing out examples of tips for building assets in infants in each of the eight categories (such as the tips for Asset 2: Positive Family Communication on pages 34–35 and for Asset 24: Enjoyment of Learning on page 172).

KEY POINTS TO MAKE

- The 40 developmental assets for infants help us understand and nurture babies' growth. The assets are a tool that help infants develop into caring, competent children.

- Almost all of the definitions start out with the word *parents*. There's a reason for this. Parents and caregivers are the primary people who build assets in infants. Explain that the words *parent* and *parents* in the workshop and in the book *What Young Children Need to Succeed* refer to an infant's primary caregiver(s). (See page 3 in that book for a more detailed explanation.)

- A lot of the definitions emphasize that the infant observes or that parents *model* behaviors, values, and attitudes. Infants learn a lot about their world through observation, and that's why it's so critical that adults model appropriate behaviors. (See pages 3–5 in *What Young Children Need to Succeed* for additional ways to talk to participants about the language used in defining and describing the assets.)

- Although these definitions place a lot of emphasis on the parents, parents cannot build assets alone. Those who aren't parents need to do what they can to support a parent. Encourage participants to link up with a family who has an infant and to build assets in *each* member of that family.

3. ASSET BUILDERS SUPPORTING ADULTS

TEACHING POINT

Like infants, parents and caregivers need support from others.

MATERIALS

- Handout #41: The Asset Builders Around You
- *What Young Children Need to Succeed*, pages 38–39

*Allow **10** minutes for this activity*

Distribute Handout #41, go over the instructions, and give participants about 5 minutes to do the exercise. When people finish, explain the importance of asset builders and support for *adults*, particularly those caring for infants. Say: **The name of Asset 3 for infants is Other Adult Relationships. The definition of this asset is: Parents have support from three or more adults and ask for help when needed. Children receive additional love and comfort from at least one adult other than their parents.**

Emphasize the definition of Asset 3 and why you think this is important. You might say: **Caring for an infant is an intensive task that can easily become overwhelming. That's why it's critical for parents of infants to have support from three or more adults. Parents need a break at times, and they need other trusted adults who can provide help and support. Babies need other caring adults in their lives, too. The love and assistance from these adults support both the baby and the parents.**

Point out some of the tips for Asset 3 (pages 38–39 of *What Young Children Need to Succeed*).

KEY POINTS TO MAKE

- Not only do infants need support from others, so do parents and caregivers.

- The more support an adult receives, the better.

- It's critical to be able to ask for help when needed. That could be calling a pediatrician in the middle of the night, asking a neighbor to pitch in, or enlisting the help of an extended family member. Parents need to know they can and should ask for this help. Other adults need to be available to give help when it's needed.

- Asset building reminds us that it's not only parents, but all of us, who have the responsibility for raising children. With children who are infants, one of the best ways for nonparents to fulfill that responsibility is to be supportive of parents.

4. FLOOR PLAY WITH INFANTS

TEACHING POINT

Playing with infants stimulates their growth and builds their assets.

MATERIALS

- Handout #13: Tips for Playing with Infants
- Several blankets
- Large assortment of toys appropriate for infants (such as rattles, balls, cloth and board books, black-and-white grasping toys, plastic mirrors, and items from infant gyms)
- *What Young Children Need to Succeed*, pages 127–128, 166–167, and 171–172

Allow **10–15 minutes** for this activity

Distribute Handout #13. Briefly highlight a couple of the key points it makes. You might say: **Infants experience rapid changes during the first 12 months of life. On this handout, you'll see tips that apply to playing with infants in three age groups: newborn–3 months, 3–7 months, and 7–12 months. No matter what type of play you're involved in, be sensitive to how the baby reacts. Follow the baby's enthusiasm. Stop when the infant gives you signals (such as turning away or fussing) that she or he is finished.**

Then have everyone sit on the floor near you. Spread out a blanket and place all the infant toys on it. Explain the importance of adults spending time on the floor with the infant. Talk about some of the toys you brought. Give examples of how participants can play with infants. Point out some of the suggestions from the handout. Feel free to let participants try some of these ideas. If your group is large, have participants form groups. Each group can sit on a blanket and discuss and handle the toys.

KEY POINTS TO MAKE

- Playing with infants stimulates their growth and builds their assets. In particular, play builds Asset 17: Creative Activities (if the play involves the arts), Asset 23: Stimulating Activity, and Asset 24: Enjoyment of Learning. Point out some of the tips found in *What Young Children Need to Succeed* for supporting these three assets in infants (pages 127–128, 166–167, and 171–172).

- Watch infants closely during play. Learn how they react when they're enjoying playing and when they tire of it. You'll see infants bat at toys, smile, and make gurgling noises when they're enjoying play. You'll see them turn their heads or close their eyes when they're done playing.

- Playing with an infant involves getting down on the floor. Imagine always having to interact with someone who towered above you! Sitting down puts you and the infant at the same level.

- Different toys stimulate infants in different ways. An infant can shake a rattle to make something happen (the baby's action brings about a noise). A teething ring puts pressure on gums where teeth are coming in and can sometimes help soothe the pain. Black-and-white toys may stimulate an infant and raise an infant's curiosity. A ball may challenge an infant's motor skills. A book gives the baby lots to look at, touch, and feel. Though infants can't read or even identify the pictures, their brains are still stimulated in many ways.

- Expect that anything you give an infant will go in the child's mouth. Don't give small toys or things with small parts to infants. Examine each toy to make sure it's safe for the mouth.

5. BUILDING ASSETS IN INFANTS

TEACHING POINT

Building assets is a positive way to ensure that infants grow up healthy.

MATERIALS
- Handout #23: Assets for Infants: A Checklist
- *What Young Children Need to Succeed*, pages 25–286
- Handout #27: 25 Ways to Build Assets in Infants

Note: If you're conducting a 60-minute workshop, distribute Handout #23 for participants to do at home and proceed with Handout #27.

Allow **5–15 minutes** for this activity

Distribute Handout #23 and give participants about 10 minutes to complete the checklist. Explain that it isn't some kind of test, but that participants can use it as a way to become more familiar with the assets and to think and talk about how assets develop in infants. Briefly discuss any areas group members identify as needing more support. Point participants to the chapters in *What Young Children Need to Succeed* that provide suggestions for building those assets.

Note: Some of the ideas on Handout #23 relate specifically to parents and/or to the infant's home setting. If your group includes out-of-home caregivers, talk about how the suggestions relate to this broader group of caregivers and how those outside the home can support parents in meeting infants' needs.

When participants finish, distribute Handout #27. Encourage them to read the handout and post it on the refrigerator, a cupboard in the childcare center, or some other place where they'll see it often.

6. The Infant's World

TEACHING POINT

When we understand an infant's world, we're better able to build assets in the infant.

MATERIALS

- Handout #42: Keeping Children Safe
- *What Young Children Need to Succeed*, page 79

*Allow **10–15** minutes for this activity*

Get down on the floor on your hands and knees. Say: **This may look a bit silly, but getting down on all fours is the best thing we can do if we want to see the world as an infant sees it.** Have participants get down on the floor and crawl around the room with you. Tell them to think of themselves as crawling infants but to use their adult minds to gather information about the room. After a few minutes, bring everyone together. Ask:

- **What did you learn about this room as you crawled around?**

- **Would this room be a good environment for an infant? Why or why not?**

- **What would make this room an ideal environment for an infant?**

Distribute Handout #42. Review the safety checklist with participants and encourage them to use it to evaluate and make any needed changes for a safer environment at home and in the childcare setting. The safety checklist includes information for keeping older children safe as well. (Page 79 of *What Young Children Need to Succeed* also suggests ways to start childproofing a home.)

KEY POINTS TO MAKE

- Notice how big everything was from a floor's-eye-view. A couch can seem like an ocean liner to an infant.

- The workshop space probably doesn't have any toys or books on the floor. Though a room strewn with toys can feel like a disaster area, infants need toys to play with at their level. The floor is the play world of infants. There need to be toys and books on the floor so babies have stimulating things to do.

- It's possible to learn a lot about human interaction with an infant by getting down on the floor. For some infants, the main interaction they have with adults is by seeing legs and feet. That's why it's important to get down on the floor, so infants can see your face and more of your body.

- When we understand an infant's world, we can build the child's assets and have more realistic expectations about how the child will grow and develop (Asset 16: Appropriate Expectations for Growth). By actually getting down on the floor and experiencing the world from an infant's point of view, we can more easily understand the baby's stage of growth and development. The more we understand infants, the better able we'll be to set expectations that challenge but don't overwhelm them.

- It's critical to childproof a room so it's safe for an infant. This builds Asset 10: Safety.

7. First Steps

TEACHING POINT

Each person has the power to make a difference in the life of an infant.

MATERIALS

- Handout #31: First Steps for Infants

Allow 5–10 minutes for this activity

Give each participant a copy of Handout #31 and allow about 5 minutes for group members to review it and circle ideas they can use to start building infants' assets. Then ask for volunteers to share what they discovered from the sheet. Invite volunteers to state one thing they intend to do to begin building assets for infants.

Close by talking about the importance of building assets in infants and how each person has the power to make a difference in the lives of an infant. You might say: **We can start building infants' assets right now. All we have to do is make the commitment to ourselves that we want to bring out the best in infants—and in all children. Each of us can make a difference by loving and supporting infants, by building assets in them and for them.**

Other Options

- If your workshop setting is in a school, childcare center, or place of worship, take a tour of an infant play area or nursery in the building. Notice whether and how the room meets infants' needs and offers a setting that can help build assets. What changes would make the space even better for infants?

- Build on participants' creativity in Activity 7. Distribute Handout #37: Easy Ideas for Building Assets in All Young Children: A Worksheet. Focus on the infant portion of the page. Encourage participants to identify more ways to build assets in infants. Emphasize that the way you build assets in infants will change as children grow. Though your discussion will focus on infants, this handout can encourage participants to begin thinking of practical ways to build assets in all children.

- Give information about parent support groups and other services in the community for people caring for infants.

Looking Ahead

At the end of the workshop, tell participants the time and place for the next workshop. You may want to ask that they read some or all of the asset-building tips in *What Young Children Need to Succeed* for the ages of the children they'll talk about in the next workshop. Suggest that they wear loose comfortable clothes for subsequent workshops, since they may be asked to sit on the floor for some of the group activities.

Workshop 3

BUILDING ASSETS IN TODDLERS

PARTICIPANTS WILL

- gain a basic understanding of the developmental assets for toddlers (ages 13 to 35 months).
- examine some of the characteristics of typical development during the toddler period.
- identify some specific ways they can begin to build assets in toddlers.

TIME

Activity	Time
1. Understanding Toddlers	10–15 minutes
2. Introducing Developmental Assets for Toddlers	10 minutes
3. The Toddler's World	10 minutes
4. Floor Play with Toddlers	10–15 minutes
5. Building Assets in Toddlers	5–15 minutes
6. Talking to Toddlers	10–15 minutes
7. Worthwhile Sayings	5–10 minutes
Total	**60–90 minutes**

RELATED SECTIONS IN *WHAT YOUNG CHILDREN NEED TO SUCCEED*

- About the Language Used in This Book, pages 3–5
- 40 Assets Toddlers Need to Succeed, pages 18–19
- Building the Assets, pages 25–286: all material under the headings "All Children" and "Toddlers"

REPRODUCIBLE HANDOUTS USED IN WORKSHOP 3

Have ready a copy of each of the following reproducible handouts for each participant:

In addition, make a single copy of the following reproducible page for yourself:

PREPARATION

Before leading this workshop, familiarize yourself thoroughly with the information on Handouts #14, #15, and #16. You will need to know this material to conduct many of the activities.

Optional: In preparation for Activity 7, create an overhead transparency with this quotation:

> **"Nothing you do for children is ever wasted."**
> —Garrison Keillor

ACTIVITIES

1. UNDERSTANDING TODDLERS

TEACHING POINT

Toddlers need support but also independence.

- Handout #14: What to Expect of Toddlers
- Handout #15: Tips for Talking with Toddlers

This is a hands-on activity to help participants understand why toddlers have difficulty sharing and get into squabbles with other children.

Say: **We're going to do an activity to give you the experience of thinking from a toddler's point of view. Listen closely to the instructions.**

Ask participants to take a coin or something else of value from their pockets or purses. Have them each find a partner and face their partners. Then say: **Imagine that you just found your item—you've never had it before and you think it's the most wonderful treasure you've ever seen. In fact, you're sure there's not another item like it anywhere in the world. If you lose it or if someone takes it from you, it will be gone forever. How will you hold this item?** Pause for a moment while group members clutch their items and ponder this.

Then continue: **Now, while guarding your item with your life, notice that your partner is holding something just as unique. You want what your partner has, too. You know it's the only item like it on earth. You're a toddler, and you _want_ that item. What will you do?** Pause for participants to decide what to do. (Most toddlers will clutch what's theirs and grab for what isn't theirs as well.)

When the exercise is over, bring the group together. Sum up the exercise by saying something like this: **The purpose of this activity was to help you experience how toddlers view life and things around them. Toddlers are just beginning to understand the concept of ownership—in terms of what belongs to _them_. If they see something they want, they think it should be theirs. They don't yet understand the concept of sharing.** Ask for any comments people would like to share about the exercise or their experiences in teaching toddlers about ownership and sharing.

Next, distribute Handouts #14 and #15. Summarize and discuss the ideas on the handouts. Encourage participants to give examples from their own observations of how toddlers move, interact, learn, and talk and how adults can communicate positively with them.

- Toddlers are at a push-pull stage. They need support, but they also need independence. They want help, but they also want to do things themselves.

- When toddlers say "mine" and "my" and refuse to share, we need to honor that. Learning about what's "mine" is a critical part of toddlers' development. They need to understand the concept of "mine" before they can learn and understand that other people have belongings, too. We need to respect what is theirs. They might use words to claim ownership ("No! Mine!"), or they might show us in other ways (for example, by grasping their blanket and refusing to let go). We can also begin to teach them how to respect other people's things. To do this we need to keep calmly telling toddlers what's theirs and what's somebody else's and stay patient as we keep inviting toddlers to give the item back to the owner. Grabbing an item away from a toddler only reinforces the idea that it's okay to grab.

- Toddlers will gradually begin to articulate what belongs to whom. For example, a toddler will say, "Daddy's shoes. Sister's shoes. My shoes." This is an important part of development.

- Expect that toddlers will hit, slap, grab, punch, poke, and bite to get something they want or to defend an object being taken away from them. Be clear that these are inappropriate behaviors, and begin to teach children how to share. For example, a caregiver might say, "No hitting. When you're angry, use your words." Don't expect toddlers to learn this skill quickly; it takes a long time. Keep teaching and reinforcing the concept of sharing over and over.

2. Introducing Developmental Assets for Toddlers

TEACHING POINT

The 40 assets help us understand and nurture the growth of toddlers.

MATERIALS

- Handout #6: 40 Assets Toddlers Need to Succeed
- *What Young Children Need to Succeed*, pages 3–5, 18–19, and 25–286

Allow 10 minutes for this activity

Distribute Handout #6 and introduce the developmental asset framework for toddlers to participants. Point out the eight asset groups and some of the specific assets and asset definitions for toddlers. Emphasize the key roles parents, families, and other primary caregivers play in toddlers' lives. Also point out that there is a copy of the asset framework for toddlers on pages 18–19 of *What Young Children Need to Succeed*.

Briefly scan that book, pointing out examples of tips for building assets in toddlers in each of the eight categories (such as the tips for Asset 9: Service to Others on page 73 and for Asset 26: Family Values Caring on pages 192–193).

KEY POINTS TO MAKE

- The 40 developmental assets for toddlers helps us understand and nurture toddlers' growth. The assets are a tool that help toddlers develop into caring, competent children.

- Almost all of the definitions start out with the word *parents*. There's a reason for this. Parents and caregivers are the primary people who build assets in toddlers. Explain that the words *parent* and *parents* in the workshop and in the book *What Young Children Need to Succeed* refer to a toddler's primary caregiver(s). (See page 3 in that book for a more detailed explanation.)

- A lot of the definitions emphasize experimenting and beginning to practice. That's how toddlers master skills and learn new things. They need to experiment. They need to practice. They need to try things.

- Limit setting is critical for this age group. Many of the definitions talk about setting appropriate boundaries and consistently reinforcing those boundaries. (See pages 3–5 in *What Young Children Need to Succeed* for additional ways to talk to participants about the language used in defining and describing the assets.)

- Although these definitions place a lot of emphasis on the parents, parents cannot build assets alone. Those who aren't parents need to do what they can to support a parent. Encourage participants to link up with a family who has a toddler and to build assets in each member of that family.

3. THE TODDLER'S WORLD

TEACHING POINT

Through communicating with toddlers, we build assets.

MATERIALS

- Reproducible #43: Words for Toddlers (1 copy, for you)
- Plastic bucket or shoe box
- Scissors
- *What Young Children Need to Succeed*, pages 33–35 and 236–238

PREPARATION

Cut out the words from the reproducible page #43: Words for Toddlers. Place the word slips in the container.

*Allow **10** minutes for this activity*

Pass around the container full of words and have each participant draw out one piece of paper. Tell participants: **For this activity you will act like toddlers. Imagine you don't know how to count with your fingers. The only three words you know are *ma*, *da*, and *no*. You need to find someone else who has a word with the same number of letters as yours. You can't use your fingers to count the letters. You can't use words to explain or ask questions. You can't show your slip of paper to anyone else.**

Allow 2–3 minutes for participants to find a partner whose word has the same number of letters. Some participants will readily figure out ways to communicate, such as saying "ma-ma-ma-ma" to indicate a four-letter word. Others may feel at a loss. Encourage group members to keep trying and be creative.

Once participants have found a partner, have them sit together. Ask participants to discuss with their partner how this activity felt for them. You might ask: **Was it frustrating? Maddening? Did you feel helpless? What does this activity tell you about how toddlers feel when they try to communicate?**

Also ask partners to discuss the joys and challenges of living with and caring for toddlers. Encourage them to share their experiences of interacting with this age group and how they feel about doing so. If people express particular frustrations, give suggestions and encourage group members to offer ideas as well.

Then ask for volunteers to share their experience with the whole group. Finish the activity by talking about the frustrations toddlers feel, using words like the following: **We've probably all heard the toddlerhood years referred to as the "terrible twos." This label probably comes from the fact that in the second year of life children say "no" a lot. They have the newly acquired ability to get into everything, and they can be demanding. Toddlers are often frustrated because they don't yet have the language skills to express their needs in words, and they don't necessarily accept limits readily. But the term "terrible twos" is really mislabeling. Toddlers are actually going through huge mental, emotional, and social growth. You can help toddlers by accepting their feelings and helping them express the feelings in appropriate ways. Teach them appropriate ways to speak and act, and model these positive behaviors in your own interactions as well. Don't forget to enjoy and celebrate the many fun moments that occur. Seeing this period of children's lives as a positive and important stage of growth can help you keep things in perspective.**

KEY POINTS TO MAKE

- Through communicating with toddlers, we build Asset 2: Positive Family Communication and Asset 33: Interpersonal Skills. Point out some of the tips found in *What Young Children Need to Succeed* for supporting these two assets in toddlers (pages 33–35 and 236–238).

- Although toddlers are learning words, their vocabularies are limited. It's important to keep learning about the new ways toddlers communicate as they develop more skills.

- It's also important to take seriously the nonverbal communication that toddlers use. They may clap, stomp, throw themselves to the floor, squeal, hit someone they want to play with, or slap someone they're mad at. Adults can show understanding, help toddlers to get their needs met, and calmly stop them when they hit or kick others. For example, if a toddler hits another child, say, "No hitting. You're mad because Tessa has your bear. Let's find another toy to share with Tessa."

- Although toddlers have a limited vocabulary, it's never too early to begin emphasizing the importance of children using their words instead of their actions. Name the feelings that you see toddlers expressing. For example, when a toddler throws herself on the floor, say, "You're really mad. Let's calm down. I want you to show me what you're mad about."

4. Floor Play with Toddlers

TEACHING POINT

Playing with toddlers stimulates their growth and builds their assets.

MATERIALS

- Handout #16: Tips for Playing with Toddlers
- Several Ping-Pong balls (enough so that small groups of 2–3 participants can have 1 ball per group)
- *What Young Children Need to Succeed,* pages 110–111, 157–159, and 268–270

Allow 10–15 minutes for this activity

Distribute Handout #16. Briefly highlight a couple of the key points it makes. You might say: **One of the best ways to spend time with a toddler is through playing. Play is the main way toddlers learn. This handout gives practical ways to play with young toddlers (those who are 13–18 months old) and older toddlers (those who are 19–35 months old).**

Then have participants form groups of two or three. Give each group a Ping-Pong ball. Ask groups to make up games using the Ping-Pong ball (examples: rolling the ball back and forth, bouncing the ball against a wall, rolling a ball between each other's legs). Afterward, point out the tips on the handout that mention beach balls and Ping-Pong balls.

Explain the importance of adults spending time playing with a toddler. Talk about some helpful toys for this age group such as blocks, simple wooden puzzles with knobs, xylophones and simple rhythm instruments, balls, dolls, large toy cars, and realistic objects (such as child-size pots and pans and other tools for home chores). Point out the importance of giving toddlers of *both* sexes opportunities to play with dolls, trucks, housekeeping toys, and blocks.

KEY POINTS TO MAKE

- Playing with toddlers stimulates their growth and builds their assets. In particular, play builds Asset 15: Positive Peer Interaction and Influence, Asset 21: Achievement Expectation and Motivation, and Asset 38: Self-Esteem. Point out some of the tips found in *What Young Children Need to Succeed* for supporting these assets in toddlers (pages 110–111, 157–159, and 268–270).

- Provide a variety of toys to build toddlers' skills. Toy mops, lawnmowers, vacuum cleaners, and trucks give toddlers the opportunity to develop the large muscles in their arms and legs. Wooden puzzles with knobs, stacking and nesting materials, pounding benches, and blocks challenge toddlers to build fine-motor skills as they manipulate their fingers and hands. Simple items such as a Ping-Pong ball can entertain and challenge a toddler. A bar of soap is such an item and a great source of enjoyment for a toddler in the bathtub. (Toddlers should never be left alone in the bathtub.)

- Allow toddlers the freedom to do what they want with objects. Often, adults step in too quickly to show toddlers how to play. Toddlers will figure out what to do with an object, just like the small groups did with a Ping-Pong ball.

- Many everyday household items make great toys for toddlers: small plastic containers and lids, pots and pans, and boxes can all be sources of fun and learning.

- When playing with a toddler, follow the child's lead. Toddlers often have clear ideas of what they want you to do. For example, a toddler may give you two blocks and want you to stack them on top of each other, give you a doll to rock, or just hand you a toy and expect you to play with it.

- Whatever toys or household items toddlers play with, make sure they are safe and age-appropriate. Trucks, cars, and other play objects need to be large enough that a child could not swallow or choke on them. There should be no small parts that could easily break off.

5. BUILDING ASSETS IN TODDLERS

TEACHING POINT

Building assets is a positive way to ensure that toddlers grow up healthy.

MATERIALS

- Handout #24: Assets for Toddlers: A Checklist
- *What Young Children Need to Succeed*, pages 25–286
- Handout #28: 25 Ways to Build Assets in Toddlers
- Handout #42: Keeping Children Safe

Note: If you're conducting a 60-minute workshop, distribute Handout #24 for participants to do at home and proceed with Handouts #28 and #42.

Allow 5–15 minutes for this activity

Distribute Handout #24 and give participants about 10 minutes to complete the checklist. Explain that it isn't some kind of test, but that participants can use it as a way to become more familiar with the assets and to think and talk about how assets develop in toddlers. Briefly discuss any areas group members identify as needing more support. Point participants to chapters in *What Young Children Need to Succeed* that provide suggestions for building these assets.

Note: Some of the ideas on Handout #24 relate specifically to parents and/or to the toddler's home setting. If your group includes out-of-home caregivers, talk about how the suggestions relate to this broader group of caregivers and how those outside the home can support parents in meeting toddlers' needs.

When participants finish, distribute Handout #42: Keeping Children Safe. Go over the handout briefly, answering questions and stressing the importance of childproofing the toddler's home and play area.

In addition, give participants Handout #28. Encourage them to read the handout and post it on the refrigerator, a cupboard in the childcare center, or some other place where they'll see it often. Emphasize that keeping toddlers safe builds Asset 10: Safety.

Note: Workshop 2 has a hands-on safety activity that can be easily adapted for use with adults who live or care for toddlers. See pages 36–37 (Activity 6: The Infant's World).

6. TALKING TO TODDLERS

TEACHING POINT

The way parents and caregivers talk impacts a toddler's development.

MATERIALS

- Handout #44: Creating Asset-Building Messages

Allow 10–15 minutes for this activity

Tell participants: **How we talk to toddlers is important. It's easy to get in the habit of saying "no" or offering negative comments like "We don't do that" or "That isn't nice." Toddlers *do* need to learn right from wrong, but we'll build more assets with positive comments.** Invite participants to suggest some positive comments for toddlers. If necessary, you might suggest some of the following:

- "You're sad. Why are you sad?"
- "It's nice to see you pet the kitty gently."
- "Playing with the lamp cord isn't safe. Play over here with me so we can play safely."
- "Yes, I like cookies too. *One* cookie is just enough for a special treat. If you're still hungry, you can have some fruit."

Distribute Handout #44 and give participants time to do the exercise. When people finish, invite volunteers to read some of the messages they wrote.

KEY POINTS TO MAKE

- The way you talk impacts a toddler's development. When you speak in positive ways, you're nurturing the toddler's assets.

- Expect toddlers to use a lot of gestures to communicate their needs. For example, they'll point to things they want or hold up their arms to be picked up.

- Pay close attention to the words toddlers use. (Common words for toddlers can include "baba" for "bottle" and "baw" for "ball." Older toddlers will use more complex language skills and say words such as "shakes" for "salt" and "blocklee" for "broccoli.") Adults should learn this language so they can understand, but use adult words for their part of the conversation. "Yes, it's time for a bottle of juice."

- Talk with toddlers. Ask them questions. With young toddlers, ask questions they can respond to with a nod (for yes), a shake of the head (for no), a grunt, or a pointed finger. With older toddlers, ask question that require more verbal responses, such as: "Do you want to go outside? Where do you want to go?" "Are you hungry? What would you like to eat?"

7. WORTHWHILE SAYINGS

TEACHING POINT

We can make a difference by building assets in toddlers.

MATERIALS

- Handout #45: Quotes About Developmental Assets
- Handout #32: First Steps for Toddlers
- **Optional:** Overhead projector and transparency you've made with the quote from Garrison Keillor

Allow 5–10 minutes for this activity

Distribute copies of Handout #45. Have group members circle two of the quotes that they find particularly meaningful. Encourage participants to post those quotes on their refrigerator at home or on a bulletin board or wall in their workplace. Emphasize the importance of building assets in toddlers.

Distribute copies of Handout #32 and encourage group members to take it home with them, review it, and circle ideas they can use to start building toddlers' assets.

Note: Workshop 2 has a more detailed "First Steps" activity that can be easily adapted for use with adults who live with or care for toddlers. See page 37.

End the session by displaying the quote from Garrison Keillor or by reading it to the group.

Say: **Garrison Keillor is right. Nothing we do for toddlers is wasted. Each time we help a toddler get dressed or eat a meal, we're building assets. Every time we get down on the floor and play with a toddler, we're building assets. Every time we place limits on a toddler who's acting in an inappropriate way, every time we show a toddler our love and support, we're building assets. So let's start today. Let's start building assets.**

OTHER OPTIONS

- Invite a childcare provider who works directly with toddlers to come and give a short presentation (5–10 minutes) to the group about his or her experience with toddlers.

- Create an activity out of Handout #37: Easy Ideas for Building Assets in All Young Children: A Worksheet. Have participants form four groups based on their experience working with or caring for children from different age groups. One group will focus on infants, one on toddlers, one on preschoolers, and one on elementary-age children. Encourage groups to look at the handout and identify more ways to build assets for their assigned age group. Then have groups report some of their ideas. Encourage participants to write the ideas they hear on their individual handouts. Then they'll have a handy list of lots of ideas for building assets in children of all ages.

- Give information about parent support groups and other services in the community for people caring for toddlers.

- Have the group brainstorm two lists: the "Terrible Twos" and the "Terrific Twos." Compare the two lists and talk about how asset builders would view each list.

LOOKING AHEAD

At the end of the workshop, tell participants the time and place for the next workshop. You may want to ask that they read some or all of the asset-building tips in *What Young Children Need to Succeed* for the ages of the children they'll talk about in the next workshop. Suggest that they wear loose comfortable clothes for subsequent workshops, since they may be asked to sit on the floor for some of the group activities.

Workshop 4

BUILDING ASSETS IN PRESCHOOLERS

PARTICIPANTS WILL

- gain a basic understanding of the developmental assets for preschoolers (ages 3 to 5 years).
- examine some of the characteristics of typical development during the preschool period.
- identify some specific ways they can begin to build assets in preschoolers.

TIME

Activity	Time
1. Understanding Preschoolers	10–15 minutes
2. Introducing Developmental Assets for Preschoolers	10 minutes
3. The Wonder of Books	5–15 minutes
4. Playtime with Preschoolers	10–15 minutes
5. Building Assets in Preschoolers	10–15 minutes
6. Superheroes in the Lives of Preschoolers	10 minutes
7. A Pledge for Children	5–10 minutes
Total	**60–90 minutes**

RELATED SECTIONS IN *WHAT YOUNG CHILDREN NEED TO SUCCEED*

- Building the Assets, pages 25–286: all material under the headings "All Children" and "Preschoolers"

Reproducible Handouts Used in Workshop 4

Have ready a copy of each of the following reproducible handouts for each participant:

Preparation

Before leading this workshop, familiarize yourself thoroughly with the information on Handouts #17, #18 and #19. You will need to know this material to conduct many of the activities.

ACTIVITIES

1. Understanding Preschoolers

TEACHING POINT

Preschoolers love to use their imagination, and they ask lots of questions.

MATERIALS

- Handout #17: What to Expect of Preschoolers
- Handout #18: Tips for Talking with Preschoolers
- A suitcase or box full of clothes, shoes, and other accessories for dramatic play (such as a hard-hat, a stethoscope, a medical smock, a tool vest, work tools, costume jewelry, purses, gloves, neckties, oven mitts, sunglasses, and so on), enough for each participant to choose 1 item

Allow 10–15 minutes for this activity

Pass around the suitcase or box. Ask participants to choose one item from it to put on. After everyone has an item, have participants find a partner. Then say something like: **Imagine that you're a preschooler. When you put on this item, who are you? What do you** do? How do you act? How do you feel? Wearing your items, what could you and your partner play together? Talk about these questions with your partner.

When the exercise is over, bring the group together and ask for volunteers to talk about what it was like to think about play from a preschooler's perspective.

Next, distribute Handouts #17 and #18. Summarize and discuss the ideas on the handouts. Encourage participants to give examples from their own observations of how preschoolers move, interact, learn, and talk and how adults can communicate positively with them.

KEY POINTS TO MAKE

- Preschoolers love to use their imagination. They like to dress up and pretend to be different people.

- While toddlers often play side by side, preschoolers begin to play *with* other children. When they "play dress up," they'll interact with the children and adults around them.

- Expect to hear a lot of questions from preschoolers. "What's this for?" "Why did you do that?" It's important to take every question seriously and to answer all questions. If you don't know the answer, say so. Let children know you'll try to find the answer. Follow through on this.

2. INTRODUCING DEVELOPMENTAL ASSETS FOR PRESCHOOLERS

TEACHING POINT

The 40 assets help us understand and nurture the growth of preschoolers.

MATERIALS

- Handout #7: 40 Assets Preschoolers Need to Succeed
- *What Young Children Need to Succeed*, pages 18–19 and 25–286

Allow **10 minutes** for this activity

Distribute Handout #7 and introduce the developmental asset framework for preschoolers to participants. Point out the asset groups and some of the specific assets and asset definitions for preschoolers. Also show participants that there is a copy of the asset framework for preschoolers on pages 18–19 of *What Young Children Need to Succeed*. Explain that the definitions for these 40 assets emphasize letting preschoolers practice and learn. (The Social Competencies assets on pages 229–253 in the participant book particularly highlight this point.)

KEY POINTS TO MAKE

- The 40 developmental assets for preschoolers help us understand and nurture preschoolers' growth. The assets are a tool that help preschoolers develop into caring, competent children.

- What's unique about the preschool definitions for the 40 developmental assets is that they show the child beginning to emerge as a separate individual. For example, compare the definitions of the Positive Values assets (Assets 26–31) for toddlers and preschoolers: For toddlers, all of the definitions begin with the word *parents*. For preschoolers, three of the asset definitions (26: Family Values Caring, 29: Family Values Honesty, and 30: Family Values Responsibility) begin by placing the emphasis on the child.

- The preschool definitions of Asset 33: Interpersonal Skills and Asset 36: Peaceful Conflict Resolution include the words *interact* and *practice*. These are important parts of being a preschooler: to interact with people and to develop skills through practice. The definitions also highlight the beginning skills that are emerging for preschoolers. For example, Asset 32: Planning and Decision Making talks about preschoolers beginning to make age-appropriate choices.

3. THE WONDER OF BOOKS

TEACHING POINT

Books build assets in many ways.

MATERIALS

- Handout #46: Your Favorite Books
- Handout #47: Picture Books That Build Assets
- *What Young Children Need to Succeed*, pages 176–179
- **Optional:** Bring some of your favorite books for preschoolers. Or bring preschool books with asset-building themes, such as those described on Handout #47.

Note: If you're conducting a 60-minute workshop, distribute Handouts #46 and #47, briefly make the key points for this activity, and proceed to Activity 4.

Allow **5–15 minutes** for this activity

Distribute Handout #46 and give participants time to do the exercise. When people finish, discuss the importance role books play in the lives of preschoolers (and children of all ages). You might say: **Reading opens up new worlds and makes a big impression on preschoolers. Children at this age love to look at lively, colorful illustrations and hear the same stories over and over. If you haven't already done so, this is an ideal time to introduce children to the library. Make reading a regular part of preschoolers' daily routine.**

Ask for volunteers to share some of their favorite books. Distribute Handout #47 and review some of the books it includes. Encourage participants to add other books to the list and to use it to select books for sharing with preschoolers. If you brought books, read aloud briefly from some of them and talk about why you enjoy reading them with preschoolers.

KEY POINTS TO MAKE

- Reading for Pleasure is Asset 25. Stories can open up new worlds to preschoolers and tap into their imagination. Stories can teach positive values, social competencies, and many of the other assets.

- Find books with vivid illustrations. Preschoolers love looking at interesting pictures.

- Find books that increase preschoolers' knowledge and understanding of nature, feelings, people, machines, and topics that interest them.

- Make time with books a positive experience. Have preschoolers sit on your lap. Ask them to tell you the story in a book. (They'll make up stories based on the pictures.) Make book time something preschoolers look forward to. This is a key for helping children develop a lifelong interest in books.

- It's also important for children to see that adults enjoy reading. It's a good idea for grown-ups to not only read *to* and *with* preschoolers but also read things of interest to adults *alongside* children. When adults set aside time to read on their own, preschoolers see firsthand that reading is an important activity in adults' lives.

4. PLAYTIME WITH PRESCHOOLERS

TEACHING POINT

Playing with preschoolers stimulates their growth and builds their assets.

MATERIALS

- Enough assorted colored lollipops so that there is 1 for you and each participant (lollipops should be solid colors, not multicolored)
- Handout #19: Tips for Playing with Preschoolers

Allow **10–15 minutes** for this activity

Give each participant a lollipop, telling the group to wait before eating them. Keep one lollipop for yourself. Introduce the activity by explaining that playing is a way preschoolers both have fun and learn. Tell participants that you're going to read them a short story. Ask them to hold up their lollipop when you read the name of its color in the story.

Read the story: **Once upon a time there were two children: a girl and a boy. The girl loved wearing purple and orange. The boy loved wearing blue and red. Whenever they got together, they would color. The boy would color circles of brown, yellow, and pink. The girl would color squares of green, blue, and purple. Sometimes the children grew tired of coloring. One day they stopped coloring and went outside where the yellow sun was shining in the blue sky on the green grass. That's when they saw a butterfly. It was orange and black. They saw a brown puppy wearing a red collar. The dog ran over to them and licked them with a slobbery, pink tongue. All this excitement made the children very, very hungry. Fortunately, the boy and girl each had a _____ lollipop.** Name the color of the lollipop you're holding. **They unwrapped their lollipops and began to eat them.**

Unwrap your lollipop and begin to eat it. Encourage everyone with lollipops of the same color to unwrap them. Then, one by one, name the different lollipop colors, asking people to unwrap and eat theirs when the color is mentioned.

As people eat their lollipops, talk about the activity. The story would capture the attention of preschool children because preschoolers love showing what they know (holding up lollipops representing their colors), hearing stories, and enjoy having a special treat.

Then distribute Handout #19. Briefly highlight a couple of the points it makes. You might say: **Playing with a preschooler is like going on an adventure. You never know when you'll encounter dinosaurs, dragons, fairies, and playful imaginary puppies! While it's important to create experiences that stimulate children's imagination, we also need to play in ways that help them develop more coordination and physical skill. Painting, building with blocks, riding a tricycle, molding dough or clay, and climbing on play equipment are just a few activities that help children develop needed skills.**

KEY POINTS TO MAKE

- Playing with preschoolers stimulates their growth and builds assets in them. Playing builds Asset 23: Stimulating Activity and Asset 24: Enjoyment of Learning, in addition to many other assets.

- Make learning fun. In this experience, identifying colors was fun. The story and interactive approach is much more effective than just showing children flash cards with different colors.

- Make learning active. In this experience, people were able to touch the colors and hold them up when they were called. Preschoolers are more engaged in learning when they participate in it by touching, seeing, hearing, smelling, and tasting.

- This activity was adult led, but a good deal of preschool play should allow the children to choose and lead the activities. Ask preschoolers what they want to play with you, and they'll come up with a lot of ideas. For example, a preschooler might want you to be a doctor and have you be the sick person. Or you'll be asked to be a big sister, a little brother, or a giant elephant. Respect children's ideas and play with them in ways that they enjoy.

5. BUILDING ASSETS IN PRESCHOOLERS

TEACHING POINT

Building assets is a positive way to ensure that preschoolers grow up healthy.

MATERIALS

- Handout #25: Assets for Preschoolers: A Checklist
- *What Young Children Need to Succeed*, pages 25–286
- Handout #29: 25 Ways to Build Assets in Preschoolers

Note: If you're conducting a 60-minute workshop, distribute Handout #25 for participants to do at home and proceed with Handout #29.

Allow **10–15 minutes** for this activity

Distribute Handout #25 and give participants about 10 minutes to complete the checklist. Explain that it isn't some kind of test, but that participants can use it as a way to become more familiar with the assets and to think and talk about how assets develop in toddlers. Briefly discuss any areas group members identify as needing more support. Point participants to chapters in *What Young Children Need to Succeed* that provide suggestions for building these assets.

Note: Some of the ideas on the handout relate specifically to parents and/or to the preschooler's home setting. If your group includes out-of-home caregivers, talk about how the suggestions relate to this broader group of caregivers and how those outside the home can support parents in meeting preschoolers' needs.

When participants finish, distribute Handout #29. Encourage them to read the handout and post it on the refrigerator, a cupboard in the childcare center or preschool, or some other place where they'll see it often.

6. SUPERHEROES IN THE LIVES OF PRESCHOOLERS

TEACHING POINT

Superheroes allow preschoolers to experiment with a positive sense of power.

MATERIALS

• *What Young Children Need to Succeed*, pages 263–266

Allow **10 minutes** for this activity

Have participants find a partner. Ask them to tell each other who their favorite superheroes were when they were children. Also ask about some of the "bad guys" that their superheroes fought. After a few minutes, bring the group together. Ask:

• **How did you feel remembering and talking about your superheroes? Why did you feel that way?**

• **Why were superheroes important to you as a child?**

• **Who are some of the superheroes for children today?**

• **How do you feel about today's superheroes for children?**

Tell the group that the interest in superheroes typically starts during the preschool years and gradually evolves into an interest in other types of heroes during later childhood and adolescence. Invite participants to discuss why superheroes are important for preschoolers. Share ideas for ways to support positive enjoyment of superheroes while discouraging negative role models. Point participants to Asset 37: Personal Power, as it relates to preschoolers (pages 263–266 in *What Young Children Need to Succeed*).

- Preschoolers watch superheroes on television, read about them, and pretend to be them in their play. All of this allows preschoolers to experiment with a positive sense of personal power. When they act like superheroes, preschoolers feel like they're in charge: they get to set the rules and control what happens.

- Superheroes also tap into a preschooler's imagination, letting the child pretend to be somebody else and see what that's like. Some of the superheroes younger preschoolers like might include animals (such as Simba and Nala from *The Lion King* or Barney and Baby Bop from the TV series *Barney & Friends*) or TV characters like the Teletubbies. Older preschoolers also choose superheroes from books, TV programs, and movies. Pokémon characters are often big hits, as are Superman, Spider-man, Batman, Princess Jasmine, and Cinderella.

- It's important to place firm boundaries on comic books, television shows, movies, and Web sites about superheroes. The content of one may be fine for preschoolers while material on others may be too sophisticated, or even scary. For example, while it's probably fine for a 3-year-old to pretend to be Batman and wear Batman under-wear or a Batman costume, movies and TV shows about Batman are generally geared to children at least age 7.

- Superheroes tap into preschooler's sense of creativity. Superheroes do things that no humans can do, and preschoolers often build on that sense of creativity. Often when preschoolers act like their superheroes, they aren't mimicking the exact behaviors. They're making up new ones and figuring out even bigger and better ways to be a superhero.

- Preschoolers may learn about gender roles through superheroes. That's one of the reasons why it's important that adults monitor which superheroes are capturing children's attention. Children will try on all sorts of roles, from the "bad guys" to the "good guys." Watch out for aggressive behavior if it goes beyond fantasy.

- When preschoolers play "house," girls may take the part of moms, grandmas, sisters, and babies while boys may take on the role of dads, grandpas, and brothers. Part of what children are doing is figuring out who they are and imitating adults and older siblings who are the same sex as they are. This helps preschoolers begin to develop a positive sense of their own gender identity. At the same time, preschoolers may sometimes decide to play the role of someone of the opposite sex. Don't be overly concerned about whatever roles, male or female, children choose to play.

- Preschoolers often play or tell stories with violent themes. During imaginary play, stuffed animals and plastic figures may die, get eaten up or thrown in the garbage, crash, or go to the hospital. Don't panic over this type of play, but be clear that violence toward *people* (such as hitting, shoving, pinching, or kicking) is not acceptable. The American Academy of Pediatrics says that a preschool-age child is too young to fully comprehend what it means to kill or to die. Shooting with sticks picked up from the ground is an entertaining form of play to a preschooler. It can build a sense of self-esteem as long as adults monitor the play and ensure that the child doesn't begin poking or throwing the stick at people.

7. A Pledge for Children

TEACHING POINT

It's important to pledge our commitment to build assets in preschoolers.

MATERIALS

- Handout #48: A Pledge to Build Children's Assets
- Handout #33: First Steps for Preschoolers

Allow 5–10 minutes for this activity

Give each participant a copy of Handout #48. Allow time for participants to read it and sign their name at the bottom. Ask for volunteers to say what they plan to do to fulfill their pledge.

Distribute copies of Handout #33 and encourage group members to take it home with them, review it, and circle ideas they can use to start building preschoolers' assets.

Note: Workshop 2 has a more detailed "First Steps" activity that can be easily adapted for use with adults who live with or care for preschoolers. See page 37.

Close by having everyone gather together and hold hands. Say something like: **We pledge our commitment to bringing out the best in preschoolers by building assets in them and for them. We can do this in simple ways. What's important is that we start and that we keep building assets every time we see a child.**

Other Options

- Invite a parent and preschooler to come demonstrate some of their favorite activities to do together.

- Give information about parent support groups and other services in the community for people caring for preschoolers.

- Create an activity out of Handout #37: Easy Ideas for Building Assets in All Young Children: A Worksheet. Have participants form four groups based on their experience working with or caring for children from different age groups. One group will focus on infants, one on toddlers, one on preschoolers, and one on elementary-age children. Encourage groups to look at the handout and identify more ways to build assets for their assigned age group. Then have groups report some of their ideas. Encourage participants to write the ideas they hear on their individual handouts. Then they'll have a handy list of lots of ideas for building assets in children of all ages.

- Have participants form pairs. One of the two can take the role of a preschooler while the other is an adult. Have partners role-play conversations with preschoolers. They can use Handout #18: Tips for Talking with Preschoolers, as a guide.

- Distribute and discuss Handout #42: Keeping Children Safe. The handout lists ways to childproof the home and play environments of infants and toddlers. Some of the items on the checklist apply to families with preschoolers as well. If your group includes parents of infants and toddlers, refer to Workshop 2 for a hands-on safety activity. See pages 36–37 (Activity 6: The Infant's World).

LOOKING AHEAD

At the end of the workshop, tell participants the time and place for the next workshop. You may want to ask that they read some or all of the asset-building tips in *What Young Children Need to Succeed* for the ages of the children they'll talk about in the next workshop. Suggest that they wear loose comfortable clothes for subsequent workshops, since they may be asked to sit on the floor for some of the group activities.

Workshop 5

BUILDING ASSETS IN ELEMENTARY-AGE CHILDREN

PARTICIPANTS WILL

- gain a basic understanding of the developmental assets for elementary-age children (ages 6 to 11 years).
- examine some of the characteristics of typical development during the elementary-age years.
- identify some specific ways they can begin to build assets in elementary-age children.

TIME

Activity	Time
1. Understanding Elementary-Age Children	10–15 minutes
2. Introducing Developmental Assets for Elementary-Age Children	10 minutes
3. The Children Around You	10 minutes
4. The Play-by-Play with Elementary-Age Children	5–15 minutes
5. Building Assets in Elementary-Age Children	10–15 minutes
6. The World of Collections	10–15 minutes
7. Asset Building in Action	5–10 minutes
Total	**60–90 minutes**

RELATED SECTIONS IN *WHAT YOUNG CHILDREN NEED TO SUCCEED*

- 40 Assets Elementary-Age Children Need to Succeed, pages 22–23
- Building the Assets, pages 25–286: all material under the headings "All Children" and "Elementary-Age Children"

Reproducible handouts used in Workshop 5

Have ready a copy of each of the following reproducible handouts for each participant:

PREPARATION

Before leading this workshop, familiarize yourself thoroughly with the information on Handouts #20, #21 and #22. You will need to know this material to conduct many of the activities.

ACTIVITIES

1. UNDERSTANDING ELEMENTARY-AGE CHILDREN

TEACHING POINT

Elementary-age children are still developing fine and gross motor skills.

MATERIALS

- 1 plastic spoon for each participant
- Bag of small marshmallows
- 3 buckets, shoe boxes, or other containers for the activity
- Handout #20: What to Expect of Elementary-Age Children
- Handout #21: Tips for Talking with Elementary-Age Children

*Allow **10–15 minutes** for this activity*

Give each participant a plastic spoon and one small marshmallow. Have participants form three groups, each with an equal number of people, and stand in single-file lines near one side of the room facing the other side. (If you don't have equal numbers of people, have groups designate a person to do the activity twice to even out the team numbers. Give those doing the activity twice an extra marshmallow.) Place a bucket or box about 10 feet away from the first person in each line.

Explain that each team is going to race against the others. Say something like: **When I say "Go," the first person in each line must place the marshmallow on the spoon. The person then must walk quickly to the bucket without running or dropping the marshmallow along the way. If the marshmallow falls, the person must pick it up, hold it in his or her hand, run back to the beginning of the line, and start again. The goal is to carry the marshmallow on the spoon all the way to the bucket, drop it into the bucket, and run back with the spoon in hand to tag the next person in line to start. The first team to finish wins the race.**

When the exercise is over, bring the group together. Explain that the point of the exercise was to emphasize that elementary-age children usually like competitive activities. Adults need to monitor these competitions so they don't end up discouraging children. Ask for any comments people would like to share.

Next, distribute Handouts #20 and #21. Summarize and discuss the ideas on the handouts. Encourage participants to give examples from their own observations of how elementary-age children move, interact, learn, and talk and how adults can communicate positively with them. Say: **The elementary-school years encompass a wide age span from 6-year-olds (kindergartners) to 11-year-olds (5th graders). The handouts give an overview of what to expect of children during this period. Some older elementary-age children are starting puberty, which means they're beginning to face issues that young teenagers face.**

You may want to suggest that participants introduce older elementary-age children who are starting puberty to *What Teens Need to Succeed: Proven, Practical Ways to Shape Your Own Future* by Peter L. Benson, Ph.D., Judy Galbraith, M.A., and Pamela Espeland (Minneapolis: Free Spirit Publishing, 1998). This book shows teenagers how to build their own assets.

KEY POINTS TO MAKE

- Children are still developing fine and gross motor skills. Fine motor skills include cutting, drawing, and manipulating small items with the fingers (for example, by stringing beads and putting together simple models). Gross motor skills are those that children need to kick a ball accurately, catch, run and zigzag up a basketball court, and do somersaults and cartwheels. Putting a marshmallow on a spoon and walking without dropping it is an activity that can help develop both kinds of physical skills in children.

- Children at this age are interested in learning and following rules for a game or competition like the one in this activity.

- Children at this age are beginning to learn how to play together as a team.

2. Introducing Developmental Assets for Elementary-Age Children

TEACHING POINT

The 40 assets help us understand and nurture the growth of elementary-age children.

MATERIALS

- Handout #8: 40 Assets Elementary-Age Children Need to Succeed
- *What Young Children Need to Succeed,* pages 22–23 and 25–286

*Allow **10** minutes for this activity*

Distribute Handout #8 and introduce the developmental asset framework for elementary-age children to participants. Point out the asset groups and some of the specific assets and asset definitions for children of this age. Also show participants that there is a copy of the asset framework for elementary-age children on pages 22–23 of *What Young Children Need to Succeed.* Explain that the definitions for these 40 assets emphasize that children are learning and practicing various skills and values.

KEY POINTS TO MAKE

- The 40 developmental assets for elementary-age children help us understand and nurture children's growth. The assets are a tool that help children develop into caring, competent teenagers and adults.

- Compare the asset definitions for preschoolers and elementary-age children. There are some significant differences. For preschoolers, the words *family* and *parents* appear in many of the definitions. For elementary-age children, the definitions focus more on the child. This does not mean that families and parents aren't important; they still are. But it recognizes that children are beginning to *internalize* many of these assets. When children internalize assets, it means they're forming their own commitments, values, and self-perceptions that provide "internal compasses" that guide their behavior and choices.

- The asset definitions have more of a school emphasis since children at this age are now spending the majority of their waking hours in school. Look at the definitions for Asset 5: Caring Out-of-Home Climate, Asset 6: Parent Involvement in Out-of-Home Situations, Asset 12: Out-of-Home Boundaries, Asset 21: Achievement Expectation and Motivation, Asset 23: Stimulating Activity and Homework, and Asset 24: Enjoyment of Learning and Bonding to School.

- For children of this age, a number of the asset definitions (such as those for Asset 17: Creative Activities and Asset 18: Out-of-Home Activities) begin to specify amounts of time that children should spend doing certain activities. What's important about this is that children need to spend a period time long enough to let them truly get involved or develop a genuine interest in the activity. Playing the piano or playing soccer can't be achieved by playing for only a few minutes at a time.

3. The Children Around You

TEACHING POINT

Asset building calls on each of us to recognize the small and large ways we can make a difference.

MATERIALS

- Handout #49: The Children You Touch

*Allow **10** minutes for this activity*

Distribute Handout #49 and give participants about 5 minutes to do the exercise. When people finish, talk about the variety of children around us all. Some of these children are more central to our lives than others. It's important, however, to make an effort to build assets in all the children we come into contact with.

KEY POINTS TO MAKE

- Adults can build children's assets in many ways. Often, asset-building acts can be small.

- While some adults may not live with children, they usually see children in the course of their everyday lives. As people begin to identify where they see children—perhaps there's a child who lives nearby or a friend who is a parent—they can begin to see that getting access to children needn't be difficult.

- Simply becoming aware of the children we see on a daily or weekly basis and doing something small—such as smiling or greeting a child by name—can make a big difference for many children over time.

4. The Play-by-Play with Elementary-Age Children

TEACHING POINT

Play is part of the "work" of children, and play can build assets.

MATERIALS

- A football, soccer ball, basketball, or softball
- A doll (such as a fashion doll or some other type of doll elementary-age children typically play with)
- 2 large sheets of paper (such as parcel paper or pages from a flip chart)
- 2 markers
- Masking tape
- Handout #22: Tips for Playing with Elementary-Age Children

Note: If you're conducting a 60-minute workshop, distribute Handout #22 and briefly highlight the key points. Then move on to Activity 5.

*Allow **5–15** minutes for this activity*

Tape two pieces of large paper to the wall side by side. Label one "Dolls" and the other "Balls." Ask for two volunteers. Give each volunteer a marker. Tell the group: **We're**

going to have a brainstorming session focused on two items: the ball and the doll. I'll hold up first one item (hold up the doll) **and then the other** (hold up the ball). **When I hold up an item, call out your ideas about what children learn or experience in playing with it. Our volunteers will write down what you say.**

If necessary, review the rules of brainstorming: People think of as many ideas as they can, and no one judges any ideas.

Hold up the ball first. After people mention a few things, hold up the doll. Continue alternating back and forth between the two items. When ideas stop flowing, stop the activity and review the lists, pulling out some of the ideas that you wish to emphasize. You might say: **Children at this age tend to play mostly with children of the same gender: boys play with boys and girls play with girls. However, older elementary-age children are becoming more aware of the opposite sex and will play chasing games. Children are beginning to participate more in team sports and clubs. They're becoming more detailed in their play. (For example, they may dress dolls in elaborate clothes, create games with complex rules, or build highly organized structures.) They're beginning to be able to do two, three, or more things at once. (For example, while infants, toddlers, preschoolers, and younger elementary-age children typically need to make a clear transition from one activity to the next, older elementary-age children have the ability to hum, watch television, and draw a picture at the same time.)**

Distribute Handout #22 and discuss any additional comments or questions that arise.

KEY POINTS TO MAKE

- Play, which is part of the "work" of children, can build assets. For example, play can build Asset 15: Positive Peer Interaction and Influence, Asset 32: Planning and Decision Making, and Asset 37: Personal Power.

- Although it's important to provide children with toys and games that are not gender specific, children still need to play in ways in which they learn about and practice gender roles. There are basic genetic differences between the sexes, and forming a healthy gender identity is the first step in forming a healthy sexual identity. It's true that both boys *and* girls can enjoy playing with trucks *and* dolls. It's also true that we want children to grow into adults who are capable of nurturing children and who have equal work and career opportunities. Yet children still need to figure out what it means to be a "boy" or a "girl."

- Learning how to play in groups and teams is an important skill for elementary-age children to master, and it's also a key part of socialization at this age. That's why organized team sports such as T-ball and soccer are important. So are clubs and activities like scouting or playing in a band. Make sure the teams and clubs children participate in emphasize cooperation, skill building, and forming healthy relationships.

- Every day, children need time to freely choose what they want to play. With our busy lifestyles, it's often easy for children's entire days to become scheduled with school and after-school activities. Children need time to invite friends over to play and to play with toys that they want to use.

5. Building Assets in Elementary-Age Children

TEACHING POINT

Building assets is a positive way to ensure that children grow up healthy.

MATERIALS

- Handout #26: Assets for Elementary-Age Children: A Checklist
- *What Young Children Need to Succeed*, pages 25–286
- Handout #30: 25 Ways to Build Assets in Elementary-Age Children

Note: If you're conducting a 60-minute workshop, distribute Handout #26 for participants to do at home and proceed with Handout #30.

*Allow **10–15 minutes** for this activity*

Distribute Handout #26 and give participants about 10 minutes to complete the checklist. Explain that it isn't some kind of test, but that participants can use it as a way to become more familiar with the assets and to think and talk about how assets develop in toddlers. Briefly discuss any areas group members identify as needing more support. Point participants to chapters in *What Young Children Need to Succeed* that provide suggestions for building these assets. Also point out the pages at the end of each asset group that include tips children can use to build their own assets (for example, see page 87).

Note: Some of the ideas on the handout relate specifically to parents and/or to the child's home setting. If your group includes teachers or out-of-home caregivers, talk about how the suggestions relate to this broader group and how those outside the home can support parents in meeting children's needs.

When participants finish, distribute Handout #30. Encourage them to read the handout and post it on the refrigerator, a bulletin board or cupboard at work, or some other place where they'll see it often.

6. The World of Collections

TEACHING POINT

Collecting is a way that children learn about their world.

MATERIALS

- 1 white file card (3" x 5") for each participant
- 1 colored (not white) file card (3" x 5") for each participant
- Pen or pencil for each participant
- *What Young Children Need to Succeed*, pages 155–187

Allow **10–15 minutes** for this activity

Give each group member two 3" x 5" cards, one white and one that's another color. On the white card, ask participants to name what they collected as a child. On the other color card, ask them to name what they collect now as an adult. Pick up all the cards. Form groups of four people. Give half of the groups the white cards and the other half the colored cards. Have groups spread out the cards so that everyone can see them and read them. Ask groups to discuss these questions:

- **What do you think about when you look at all these cards in front of you? Why?**

- **Why do you collect things?**

- **How are the things you collect and the way you collect them now different from when you were a child?**

- **How do collections change as children become older?**

- **What's more exciting to collect: things that are free or things that cost money? Why?**

- **How do you feel about the things that children collect today?**

- **What does a certain type of collection say about a person?**

Bring people back together. Point out that elementary-age children are at the age when they begin to collect things. Discuss the importance of collections in helping children investigate and learn and in giving children a sense of ownership.

KEY POINTS TO MAKE

- Collecting is a way that children learn about their world and master information. Collecting builds the Commitment to Learning assets (Assets 21–25). For example, collecting rocks or leaves is a way that children learn more about nature.

- Children enjoy collecting things because they like to learn a lot about a particular item or subject. For example, children collect stamps because they can learn about different countries (if they collect international stamps) or about many aspects of their own culture (if they collect domestic stamps).

- Collecting things gives children an opportunity to manipulate objects. For instance, they like to see what happens if they color with markers on a rock or hit two rocks together. Collections give children the chance to explore and investigate.

- Children also collect things because it gives them a sense of ownership. Some children are natural collectors.

- Younger children are often more interested in the quantity than in the specific qualities of things collected. If you ask a 7-year-old which rock in his collection is his favorite, he'll most likely say, "I like all of them." Older children begin to get more interested in specific qualities of the different items. When asked about her favorite baseball card, an 11-year-old may tell you something like, "Mark McGwire because he hit 70 home runs in 1998, and he broke the all-time record."

7. ASSET BUILDING IN ACTION

TEACHING POINT

Each person has the potential to build assets.

MATERIALS

- Handout #50: Adding Up Your Asset-Building Potential
- Handout #34: First Steps for Elementary-Age Children

*Allow **5–10 minutes** for this activity*

Give each participant a copy of Handout #50. Give them time to fill it out. Then ask for volunteers to share what they discovered from the sheet.

Distribute copies of Handout #34 and encourage group members to take it home with them, review it, and circle ideas they can use to start building elementary-age children's assets.

Close by affirming people's interest in asset building and for choosing one way to begin building assets. Thank them for being interested in children and for their commitment in wanting to bring out the best in children.

Note: Workshop 2 has a more detailed "First Steps" activity that can be easily adapted for use with adults who live with or care for elementary-age children. See page 37.

OTHER OPTIONS

- Create an activity out of Handout #37: Easy Ideas for Building Assets in All Young Children: A Worksheet. Have participants form four groups based on their experience working with or caring for children from different age groups. One group will focus on infants, one on toddlers, one on preschoolers, and one on elementary-age children. Encourage groups to look at the handout and identify more ways to build assets for their assigned age group. Then have groups report some of their ideas. Encourage participants to write the ideas they hear on their individual handouts. Then they'll have a handy list of lots of ideas for building assets in children of all ages.

- Invite a person who volunteers with elementary-age children to come in and talk about why he or she volunteers.

- Have a list of places in the community participants can contact to volunteer with this age group. Include schools, scouting organizations, parks and recreation activities, the library, places of worship, family shelters, and so on.

- Give information about parent support groups and other services in the community for people caring for elementary-age children.

- Ask a music teacher or club leader who works with 1st, 2nd, or 3rd graders to come in with two or three children who can tell the group about some of their interests. Encourage people in the group to ask the children questions.

- Ask three older elementary-age children (ages 10 and 11) to come in and speak to the group about what activities they like and what they enjoy doing. Again, encourage people in the group to ask the children questions.

- Distribute and discuss Handout #42: Keeping Children Safe. The handout lists ways to childproof the home and play environments of infants and toddlers. Some of the items on the checklist apply to families with preschoolers. If your group includes parents of infants, toddlers, and preschoolers, refer to Workshop 2 for a hands-on safety activity. See pages 36–37 (Activity 6: The Infant's World).

LOOKING AHEAD

If you'll be conducting other workshops, tell participants the time and place for the next one. You may want to ask that they read some or all of the asset-building tips in *What Young Children Need to Succeed* for the ages of the children they'll talk about in the next workshop. Suggest that they wear loose comfortable clothes for subsequent workshops, since they may be asked to sit on the floor for some of the group activities.

REPRODUCIBLE PAGES

40 DEVELOPMENTAL ASSETS FOR 6TH GRADERS

In a survey of 9,861 6th graders in 213 cities and towns across the United States during the 1996–1997 school year, Search Institute researchers found the following percentages of 6th graders who reported having each of the 40 developmental assets:

CATEGORY	ASSET NAME AND DEFINITION

EXTERNAL ASSETS

Support

1. **Family Support.** Kids feel loved and supported in their family—79%.
2. **Positive Family Communication.** Kids turn to their parents for advice and support. They have frequent, in-depth conversations with each other on a variety of topics. Parents are approachable and available when kids want to talk—40%.
3. **Other Adult Relationships.** Kids know other adults besides their parents they can turn to for advice and support. They have frequent, in-depth conversations with them. Ideally, three or more adults play this role in their lives—41%.
4. **Caring Neighborhood.** Kids feel that their neighbors support them, encourage them, and care about them—50%.
5. **Caring School Climate.** Kids feel that their school supports them, encourages them, and cares about them—38%.
6. **Parent Involvement in Schooling.** Parents are actively involved in helping kids succeed in school—45%.

Empowerment

7. **Community Values Youth.** Kids perceive that adults in the community value young people—33%.
8. **Youth as Resources.** Kids are given useful roles in the community—36%.
9. **Service to Others.** Kids serve in the community one or more hours per week—61%.
10. **Safety.** Kids feel safe at home, at school, and in their neighborhood—45%.

Boundaries and Expectations

11. **Family Boundaries.** Parents set clear rules and consequences for their kids' behavior. They monitor their children's whereabouts—49%.
12. **School Boundaries.** Schools set clear rules and consequences for student behavior—70%.
13. **Neighborhood Boundaries.** Neighbors take responsibility for monitoring young people's behavior—59%.
14. **Adult Role Models.** Parents and other adults model positive, responsible behavior—35%.
15. **Positive Peer Influence.** Children's best friends model responsible behavior. They are a good influence. They do well in school and stay away from risky behaviors such as alcohol and other drug use—82%.
16. **High Expectations.** Parents and teachers encourage kids to do well—59%.

Constructive Use of Time

17. **Creative Activities.** Kids spend three or more hours per week in lessons or practice in music, theater, or other arts—23%.
18. **Youth Programs.** Kids spend three or more hours each week in sports, clubs, or organizations at school and/or in the community—57%.
19. **Religious Community.** Kids spend one or more hours each week in religious services or participating in spiritual activities—72%.
20. **Time at Home.** Kids go out with friends "with nothing special to do" two or fewer nights each week—57%.

INTERNAL ASSETS

Commitment to Learning

21. **Achievement Motivation.** Kids are motivated to do well in school—70%.
22. **School Engagement.** Kids are actively engaged in learning—66%.
23. **Homework.** Kids do at least one hour of homework every school day—43%.
24. **Bonding to School.** Kids care about their school—64%.
25. **Reading for Pleasure.** Kids read for pleasure three or more hours per week—33%.

Positive Values

26. **Caring.** Kids place high value on helping other people—56%.
27. **Equality and Social Justice.** Kids place high value on promoting equality and reducing hunger and poverty—59%.
28. **Integrity.** Kids act on their convictions and stand up for their beliefs—63%.
29. **Honesty.** Kids tell the truth even when it's not easy—73%.
30. **Responsibility.** Kids accept and take personal responsibility for their actions and decisions—65%.
31. **Restraint.** Kids believe that it's important not to be sexually active or to use alcohol or other drugs—71%.

Social Competencies

32. **Planning and Decision Making.** Kids know how to plan ahead and make choices—31%.
33. **Interpersonal Competence.** Kids have empathy, sensitivity, and friendship skills—47%.
34. **Cultural Competence.** Kids know and are comfortable with people of different cultural, racial, and/or ethnic backgrounds—41%.
35. **Resistance skills.** Kids can resist negative peer pressure and avoid dangerous situations—49%.
36. **Peaceful Conflict Resolution.** Kids seek to resolve conflict nonviolently—54%.

Positive Identity

37. **Personal Power.** Kids feel that they have control over many things that happen to them—40%.
38. **Self-Esteem.** Kids feel good about themselves—52%.
39. **Sense of Purpose.** Kids believe that their life has a purpose—57%.
40. **Positive View of Personal Future.** Kids are optimistic about their own future—72%.

THE POWER OF DEVELOPMENTAL ASSETS*

MORE ASSETS MEAN FEWER PROBLEM BEHAVIORS

Search Institute researchers found that the more assets a young person has, the *less* likely it is that the child will engage in risky behavior. These charts show examples of this for two types of problem behavior among 6th graders:

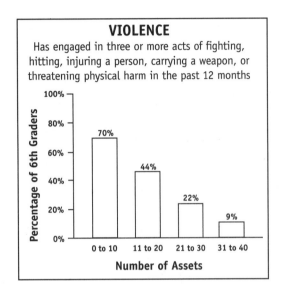

VIOLENCE
Has engaged in three or more acts of fighting, hitting, injuring a person, carrying a weapon, or threatening physical harm in the past 12 months

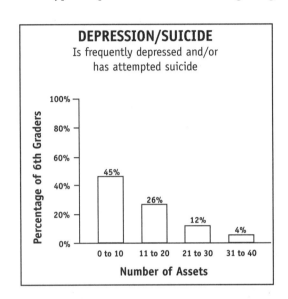

DEPRESSION/SUICIDE
Is frequently depressed and/or has attempted suicide

MORE ASSETS MEAN MORE POSITIVE BEHAVIORS

Researchers also found that the more assets a young person has, the *more* likely it is that the child will engage in positive behaviors—called *thriving indicators*. These charts show examples of this for two types of positive behavior among 6th graders:

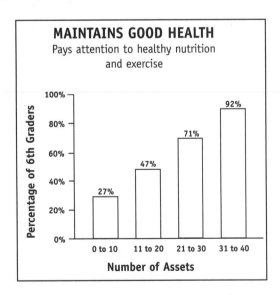

MAINTAINS GOOD HEALTH
Pays attention to healthy nutrition and exercise

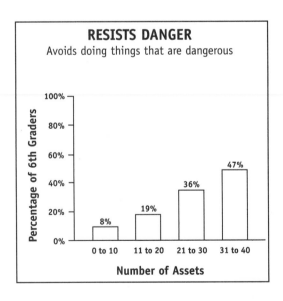

RESISTS DANGER
Avoids doing things that are dangerous

*These statistics are based on surveys of 9,861 6th graders in 213 cities and towns across the United States during the 1996–1997 school year. Search Institute found that similar statistical patterns hold true for young people in grades 7–12.

THE POWER OF ASSETS TO PROTECT 6TH GRADERS

MORE ASSETS MEAN LESS RISKY BEHAVIOR

6th graders who report more assets are *less* likely to report engaging in risky and dangerous behaviors. Search Institute has measured 24 of these behaviors, which it calls *risky behaviors.* In a survey of 9,861 6th graders in 213 cities and towns across the United States during the 1996–1997 school year, Search Institute researchers found the following percentages of 6th graders who reported engaging in each of the risky behaviors:

1. **Hitting.** 6th grader hit someone one or more times in the last 12 months—44%.
2. **Riding with a Driver Under the Influence.** 6th grader rode one or more times in the last 12 months with a driver who had been drinking alcohol—31%.
3. **Gambling.** 6th grader gambled one or more times in the last 12 months—31%.
4. **Group Fighting.** 6th grader has been in a group fight one or more times in the last 12 months—27%.
5. **Threat of Violence.** 6th grader threatened physical harm to someone one or more times in the last 12 months—27%.
6. **Shoplifting.** 6th grader has shoplifted one or more times in the last 12 months—19%.
7. **Physical Harm.** 6th grader physically hurt someone one or more times in the last 12 months—14%.
8. **School Truancy.** 6th grader skipped school one or more times in the last 4 weeks—14%.
9. **Eating Disorder.** 6th grader has engaged in bulimic or anorexic behaviors—14%.
10. **Alcohol Use.** 6th grader used alcohol one or more times in the last 30 days—13%.
11. **Inhalant Use.** 6th grader sniffed or inhaled substances to get high one or more times in the last 12 months—13%.
12. **Vandalism.** 6th grader committed vandalism one or more times in the last 12 months—13%.
13. **Trouble with Police.** 6th grader got into trouble with the police one or more times in the last 12 months—13%.
14. **Attempted Suicide.** 6th grader has attempted suicide one or more times—12%.
15. **Depression.** 6th grader has felt sad or depressed most or all of the time in the last month—11%.
16. **Carrying a Weapon.** 6th grader carried a weapon for protection one or more times in the last 12 months—10%.
17. **Drunkenness.** 6th grader got drunk once or more in the last two weeks—10%.
18. **Tobacco Use.** 6th grader smoked a cigarette one or more times in the last 30 days—10%.
19. **Sexual Intercourse.** 6th grader has had sexual intercourse one or more times—8%.
20. **Smokeless Tobacco Use.** 6th grader used smokeless tobacco one or more times in the last 12 months—5%.
21. **Weapon Use.** 6th grader used a weapon to get something from a person one or more times in the last 12 months—4%.
22. **Marijuana Use.** 6th grader used marijuana one or more times in the last 12 months—4%.
23. **Other Drug Use.** 6th grader used other illicit drugs (such as cocaine, LSD, PCP or angel dust, heroin, or amphetamines) one or more times in the last 12 months—4%.
24. **Driving Under the Influence.** 6th grader drove one or more times in the last 12 months after drinking alcohol—2%.

6TH GRADERS ACTING IN POSITIVE WAYS

MORE ASSETS MEAN MORE POSITIVE BEHAVIOR

6th graders who have more assets are *more* likely to report indicators of positive development. Search Institute has measured 8 of these positive behaviors, which it calls *thriving indicators.* In a survey of 9,861 6th graders in 213 cities and towns across the United States during the 1996–1997 school year, Search Institute researchers found the following percentages of 6th graders who reported each of the thriving indicators:

1. **Helps Others.** 6th grader helps friends or neighbors one or more hours per week—86%.

2. **Overcomes Adversity.** 6th grader does not give up when things get difficult—70%.

3. **Exhibits Leadership.** 6th grader has been a leader of a group or an organization in the last 12 months—65%.

4. **Values Diversity.** 6th grader places high importance on getting to know people of other racial/ethnic groups—64%.

5. **Maintains Good Health.** 6th grader pays attention to healthy nutrition and exercise—61%.

6. **Delays Gratification.** 6th grader saves money for something special rather than spending it all right away—52%.

7. **Resists Danger.** 6th grader avoids doing things that are dangerous—29%.

8. **Succeeds in School.** 6th grader gets mostly A's on report card—24%.

40 ASSETS INFANTS NEED TO SUCCEED

(Birth to 12 Months) Search Institute has identified a framework of 40 developmental assets for infants that blends the research on assets for 12- to 18-year-olds with the extensive literature on child development.

CATEGORY	ASSET NAME AND DEFINITION

EXTERNAL ASSETS

Support

1. **Family Support.** Family life provides high levels of love and support.
2. **Positive Family Communication.** Parents communicate with infants in positive ways. Parents respond immediately to infants and respect their needs.
3. **Other Adult Relationships.** Parents have support from three or more adults and ask for help when needed. Children receive additional love and comfort from at least one adult other than their parents.
4. **Caring Neighborhood.** Children experience caring neighbors.
5. **Caring Out-of-Home Climate.** Children are in caring, encouraging environments outside the home.
6. **Parent Involvement in Out-of-Home Situations.** Parents are actively involved in communicating infants' needs to caretakers and others in situations outside the home.

Empowerment

7. **Community Values Children.** The family places infants at the center of family life. Other adults in the community value and appreciate infants.
8. **Children Are Given Useful Roles.** The family involves infants in family life.
9. **Service to Others.** Parents serve others in the community.
10. **Safety.** Children have safe environments at home, in out-of-home settings, and in the neighborhood. This includes childproofing these environments.

Boundaries and Expectations

11. **Family Boundaries.** Parents are aware of infants' preferences and adapt the environment and schedule to suit infants' needs. Parents begin setting limits as infants become mobile.
12. **Out-of-Home Boundaries.** Childcare settings and other out-of-home environments have clear rules and consequences for older infants and consistently provide all infants with appropriate stimulation and enough rest.
13. **Neighborhood Boundaries.** Neighbors take responsibility for monitoring and supervising children's behavior as they begin to play and interact outside the home.
14. **Adult Role Models.** Parents and other adults model positive, responsible behavior.
15. **Positive Peer Interaction and Influence.** Infants observe siblings and other children interacting in positive ways. They have opportunities to interact with children of various ages.
16. **Appropriate Expectations for Growth.** Parents have realistic expectations for children's development at this age. Parents encourage development without pushing children beyond their own pace.

Constructive Use of Time

17. **Creative Activities.** Parents expose infants to music, art, or other creative aspects of the environment each day.
18. **Out-of-Home Activities.** Parents expose children to limited but stimulating situations outside the home. The family keeps children's needs in mind when attending events.
19. **Religious Community.** The family regularly attends religious programs or services while keeping children's needs in mind.
20. **Positive, Supervised Time at Home.** Parents supervise children at all times and provide predictable, enjoyable routines at home.

INTERNAL ASSETS

Commitment to Learning

21. **Achievement Expectation and Motivation.** Family members are motivated to do well at work, at school, and in the community, and model their motivation for children.
22. **Children Are Engaged in Learning.** Parents and family members model responsive and attentive attitudes at work, at school, in the community, and at home.
23. **Stimulating Activity and Homework.** Parents encourage children to explore and provide stimulating toys that match children's emerging skills. Parents are sensitive to children's dispositions, preferences, and level of development.
24. **Enjoyment of Learning and Bonding to School.** Parents enjoy learning and model this through their own learning activities.
25. **Reading for Pleasure.** Parents read to infants in enjoyable ways every day.

Positive Values

26. **Family Values Caring.** Parents convey their beliefs about helping others by modeling their helping behaviors.
27. **Family Values Equality and Social Justice.** Parents place a high value on promoting social equality, religious tolerance, and reducing hunger and poverty while modeling these beliefs for children.
28. **Family Values Integrity.** Parents act on their convictions, stand up for their beliefs, and communicate and model this in the family.
29. **Family Values Honesty.** Parents tell the truth and convey their belief in honesty through their actions.
30. **Family Values Responsibility.** Parents accept and take personal responsibility.
31. **Family Values Healthy Lifestyle.** Parents love children, setting the foundation for infants to develop healthy attitudes and beliefs about relationships. Parents model, monitor, and teach the importance of good health habits, and provide good nutritional choices and adequate rest and playtime.

Social Competencies

32. **Planning and Decision Making.** Parents make all safety and care decisions for children and model safe behavior. As children become more independently mobile, parents allow them to make simple choices.
33. **Interpersonal Skills.** Parents model positive, constructive interactions with other people. Parents accept and are responsive to how infants express their feelings, seeing those expressions as cues to infants' needs.
34. **Cultural Competence.** Parents know and are comfortable with people of different cultural, racial, and/or ethnic backgrounds, and model this to children.
35. **Resistance Skills.** Parents model resistance skills through their own behavior.
36. **Peaceful Conflict Resolution.** Parents behave in acceptable, nonviolent ways and assist children in developing these skills by helping them solve problems when they're faced with challenging or frustrating circumstances.

Positive Identity

37. **Personal Power.** Parents feel they have control over things that happen in their own lives and model coping skills, demonstrating healthy ways to deal with frustrations and challenges. Parents respond to children so children begin to learn that they have influence over their immediate surroundings.
38. **Self-Esteem.** Parents create an environment where children can develop positive self-esteem, giving children appropriate, positive feedback and reinforcement about their skills and competencies.
39. **Sense of Purpose.** Parents report that their lives have purpose and demonstrate these beliefs through their behaviors. Infants are curious about the world around them.
40. **Positive View of Personal Future.** Parents are hopeful and positive about their personal future and work to provide a positive future for children.

40 ASSETS TODDLERS NEED TO SUCCEED

(Ages 13 to 35 Months) Search Institute has identified a framework of 40 developmental assets for toddlers that blends the research on assets for 12- to 18-year-olds with the extensive literature on child development.

CATEGORY		ASSET NAME AND DEFINITION
EXTERNAL ASSETS	**Support**	1. **Family Support.** Family life provides high levels of love and support. 2. **Positive Family Communication.** Parents communicate with toddlers in positive ways. Parents respond to toddlers in a reasonable amount of time and respect their needs. 3. **Other Adult Relationships.** Parents have support from three or more adults and ask for help when needed. Children receive additional love and comfort from at least one adult other than their parents. 4. **Caring Neighborhood.** Children experience caring neighbors. 5. **Caring Out-of-Home Climate.** Children are in caring, encouraging environments outside the home. 6. **Parent Involvement in Out-of-Home Situations.** Parents are actively involved in helping toddlers succeed in situations outside the home. Parents communicate toddlers' needs to caretakers outside the home.
	Empower-ment	7. **Community Values Children.** The family places toddlers at the center of family life and recognizes the need to set limits for toddlers. Other adults in the community value and appreciate toddlers. 8. **Children Are Given Useful Roles.** The family involves toddlers in family life. 9. **Service to Others.** Parents serve others in the community. 10. **Safety.** Children have safe environments at home, in out-of-home settings, and in the neighborhood. This includes childproofing these environments.
	Boundaries and Expectations	11. **Family Boundaries.** Parents are aware of toddlers' preferences and adapt the environment to suit toddlers' needs. Parents set age-appropriate limits for toddlers. 12. **Out-of-Home Boundaries.** Childcare settings and other out-of-home environments have clear rules and consequences to protect toddlers while consistently providing appropriate stimulation and enough rest. 13. **Neighborhood Boundaries.** Neighbors take responsibility for monitoring and supervising children's behavior as they begin to play and interact outside the home. 14. **Adult Role Models.** Parents and other adults model positive, responsible behavior. 15. **Positive Peer Interaction and Influence.** Toddlers observe siblings and other children interacting in positive ways. They have opportunities to interact with children of various ages. 16. **Appropriate Expectations for Growth.** Parents have realistic expectations for children's development at this age. Parents encourage development without pushing children beyond their own pace.
	Constructive Use of Time	17. **Creative Activities.** Parents expose toddlers to music, art, or other creative age-appropriate activities each day. 18. **Out-of-Home Activities.** Parents expose children to limited but stimulating situations outside the home. The family keeps children's needs in mind when attending events. 19. **Religious Community.** The family regularly attends religious programs or services while keeping children's needs in mind. 20. **Positive, Supervised Time at Home.** Parents supervise children at all times and provide predictable, enjoyable routines at home.
INTERNAL ASSETS	**Commitment to Learning**	21. **Achievement Expectation and Motivation.** Family members are motivated to do well at work, at school, and in the community, and model their motivation for children. 22. **Children Are Engaged in Learning.** Parents and family members model responsive and attentive attitudes at work, at school, in the community, and at home. 23. **Stimulating Activity and Homework.** Parents encourage children to explore and provide stimulating toys that match children's emerging skills. Parents are sensitive to children's dispositions, preferences, and level of development. 24. **Enjoyment of Learning and Bonding to School.** Parents enjoy learning and express this through their own learning activities. 25. **Reading for Pleasure.** Parents read to toddlers every day and find ways for toddlers to participate in enjoyable reading experiences.
	Positive Values	26. **Family Values Caring.** Parents convey their beliefs about helping others by modeling their helping behaviors. 27. **Family Values Equality and Social Justice.** Parents place a high value on promoting social equality, religious tolerance, and reducing hunger and poverty while modeling these beliefs for children. 28. **Family Values Integrity.** Parents act on their convictions, stand up for their beliefs, and communicate and model this in the family. 29. **Family Values Honesty.** Parents tell the truth and convey their belief in honesty through their actions. 30. **Family Values Responsibility.** Parents accept and take personal responsibility. 31. **Family Values Healthy Lifestyle.** Parents love children, setting the foundation for toddlers to develop healthy attitudes and beliefs about relationships. Parents model, monitor, and teach the importance of good health habits, and provide good nutritional choices and adequate rest and playtime.
	Social Competencies	32. **Planning and Decision Making.** Parents make all safety and care decisions for children and model safe behavior. As children become more independently mobile, parents allow them to make simple choices. 33. **Interpersonal Skills.** Parents model positive, constructive interactions with other people. Parents accept and are responsive to how toddlers use actions and words to express their feelings, seeing those expressions as cues to toddlers' needs. 34. **Cultural Competence.** Parents know and are comfortable with people of different cultural, racial, and/or ethnic backgrounds, and model this to children. 35. **Resistance Skills.** Parents model resistance skills through their own behavior. Parents aren't overwhelmed by toddlers' needs and demonstrate appropriate resistance skills. 36. **Peaceful Conflict Resolution.** Parents behave in acceptable, nonviolent ways and assist children in developing these skills by helping them solve problems when they're faced with challenging or frustrating circumstances.
	Positive Identity	37. **Personal Power.** Parents feel they have control over things that happen in their own lives and model coping skills, demonstrating healthy ways to deal with frustrations and challenges. Parents respond to children so children begin to learn that they have influence over their immediate surroundings. 38. **Self-Esteem.** Parents create an environment where children can develop positive self-esteem, giving children appropriate, positive feedback and reinforcement about their skills and competencies. 39. **Sense of Purpose.** Parents report that their lives have purpose and model these beliefs through their behaviors. Children are curious and explore the world around them. 40. **Positive View of Personal Future.** Parents are hopeful and positive about their personal future and work to provide a positive future for children.

40 ASSETS PRESCHOOLERS NEED TO SUCCEED

(Ages 3 to 5 Years) Search Institute has identified a framework of 40 developmental assets for preschoolers that blends the research on assets for 12- to 18-year-olds with the extensive literature on child development.

CATEGORY	ASSET NAME AND DEFINITION

EXTERNAL ASSETS

Support

1. **Family Support.** Family life provides high levels of love and support.
2. **Positive Family Communication.** Parents and preschoolers communicate positively. Preschoolers seek out parents for help with difficult tasks or situations.
3. **Other Adult Relationships.** Preschoolers have support from at least one adult other than their parents. Their parents have support from people outside the home.
4. **Caring Neighborhood.** Children experience caring neighbors.
5. **Caring Out-of-Home Climate.** Children are in caring, encouraging environments outside the home.
6. **Parent Involvement in Out-of-Home Situations.** Parents are actively involved in helping preschoolers succeed in situations outside the home. Parents communicate preschoolers' needs to caretakers outside the home.

Empowerment

7. **Community Values Children.** Parents and other adults in the community value and appreciate preschoolers.
8. **Children Are Given Useful Roles.** Parents and other adults create ways preschoolers can help out and gradually include preschoolers in age-appropriate tasks.
9. **Service to Others.** The family serves others in the community together.
10. **Safety.** Preschoolers have safe environments at home, in out-of-home settings, and in the neighborhood. This includes childproofing these environments.

Boundaries and Expectations

11. **Family Boundaries.** The family has clear rules and consequences. The family monitors preschoolers and consistently demonstrates appropriate behavior through modeling and limit setting.
12. **Out-of-Home Boundaries.** Childcare settings and other out-of-home environments have clear rules and consequences to protect preschoolers while consistently providing appropriate stimulation and enough rest.
13. **Neighborhood Boundaries.** Neighbors take responsibility for monitoring and supervising children's behavior as they begin to play and interact outside the home.
14. **Adult Role Models.** Parents and other adults model positive, responsible behavior.
15. **Positive Peer Interaction and Influence.** Preschoolers are encouraged to play and interact with other children in safe, well-supervised settings.
16. **Appropriate Expectations for Growth.** Adults have realistic expectations for children's development at this age. Parents, caregivers, and other adults encourage children to achieve and develop their unique talents.

Constructive Use of Time

17. **Creative Activities.** Preschoolers participate in music, art, dramatic play, or other creative activities each day.
18. **Out-of-Home Activities.** Preschoolers interact in stimulating ways with children outside the family. The family keeps preschoolers' needs in mind when attending events.
19. **Religious Community.** The family regularly attends religious programs or services while keeping children's needs in mind.
20. **Positive, Supervised Time at Home.** Preschoolers are supervised by an adult at all times. Preschoolers spend most evenings and weekends at home with their parents in predictable, enjoyable routines.

INTERNAL ASSETS

Commitment to Learning

21. **Achievement Expectation and Motivation.** Parents and other adults convey and reinforce expectations to do well at work, at school, in the community, and within the family.
22. **Children Are Engaged in Learning.** Parents and family members model responsive and attentive attitudes at work, at school, in the community, and at home.
23. **Stimulating Activity and Homework.** Parents encourage children to explore and provide stimulating toys that match children's emerging skills. Parents are sensitive to children's dispositions, preferences, and level of development.
24. **Enjoyment of Learning and Bonding to School.** Parents and other adults enjoy learning and engage preschoolers in learning activities.
25. **Reading for Pleasure.** Adults read to preschoolers for at least 30 minutes over the course of a day, encouraging preschoolers to participate.

Positive Values

26. **Family Values Caring.** Preschoolers are encouraged to express sympathy for someone who is distressed and begin to develop a variety of helping behaviors.
27. **Family Values Equality and Social Justice.** Parents place a high value on promoting social equality, religious tolerance, and reducing hunger and poverty while modeling these beliefs for children.
28. **Family Values Integrity.** Parents act on their convictions, stand up for their beliefs, and communicate and model this in the family.
29. **Family Values Honesty.** Preschoolers learn the difference between telling the truth and lying.
30. **Family Values Responsibility.** Preschoolers learn that their actions affect other people.
31. **Family Values Healthy Lifestyle.** Parents and other adults model, monitor, and teach the importance of good health habits. Preschoolers begin to learn healthy sexual attitudes and beliefs as well as respect for others.

Social Competencies

32. **Planning and Decision Making.** Preschoolers begin to make simple choices, solve simple problems, and develop simple plans at age-appropriate levels.
33. **Interpersonal Skills.** Preschoolers play and interact with other children and adults. They freely express their feelings and learn to put these feelings into words. Parents and other adults model and teach empathy.
34. **Cultural Competence.** Preschoolers are exposed in positive ways to information about and to people of different cultural, racial, and/or ethnic backgrounds.
35. **Resistance Skills.** Preschoolers are taught to resist participating in inappropriate or dangerous behavior.
36. **Peaceful Conflict Resolution.** Parents and other adults model positive ways to resolve conflicts. Preschoolers are taught and begin to practice nonviolent, acceptable ways to deal with challenging and frustrating situations.

Positive Identity

37. **Personal Power.** Parents feel they have control over things that happen in their own lives and model coping skills, demonstrating healthy ways to deal with frustrations and challenges. Parents respond to children so children begin to learn that they have influence over their immediate surroundings.
38. **Self-Esteem.** Parents create an environment where children can develop positive self-esteem, giving children appropriate, positive feedback and reinforcement about their skills and competencies.
39. **Sense of Purpose.** Parents report that their lives have purpose and model these beliefs through their behaviors. Children are curious and explore the world around them.
40. **Positive View of Personal Future.** Parents are hopeful and positive about their personal future and work to provide a positive future for children.

40 ASSETS ELEMENTARY-AGE CHILDREN NEED TO SUCCEED

(Ages 6 to 11 Years) Search Institute has identified a framework of 40 developmental assets for elementary-age children that blends the research on assets for 12- to 18-year-olds with the extensive literature on child development.

CATEGORY	ASSET NAME AND DEFINITION

EXTERNAL ASSETS

Support

1. **Family Support.** Family life provides high levels of love and support.
2. **Positive Family Communication.** Parents and children communicate positively. Children are willing to seek advice and counsel from their parents.
3. **Other Adult Relationships.** Children have support from adults other than their parents.
4. **Caring Neighborhood.** Children experience caring neighbors.
5. **Caring Out-of-Home Climate.** School and other activities provide caring, encouraging environments for children.
6. **Parent Involvement in Out-of-Home Situations.** Parents are actively involved in helping children succeed in school and in other situations outside the home.

Empowerment

7. **Community Values Children.** Children feel that the family and community value and appreciate children.
8. **Children Are Given Useful Roles.** Children are included in age-appropriate family tasks and decisions and are given useful roles at home and in the community.
9. **Service to Others.** Children serve others in the community with their family or in other settings.
10. **Safety.** Children are safe at home, at school, and in the neighborhood.

Boundaries and Expectations

11. **Family Boundaries.** The family has clear rules and consequences and monitors children's activities and whereabouts.
12. **Out-of-Home Boundaries.** Schools and other out-of-home environments provide clear rules and consequences.
13. **Neighborhood Boundaries.** Neighbors take responsibility for monitoring children's behavior.
14. **Adult Role Models.** Parents and other adults model positive, responsible behavior.
15. **Positive Peer Interaction and Influence.** Children interact with other children who model responsible behavior and have opportunities to play and interact in safe, well-supervised settings.
16. **Appropriate Expectations for Growth.** Adults have realistic expectations for children's development at this age. Parents, caregivers, and other adults encourage children to achieve and develop their unique talents.

Constructive Use of Time

17. **Creative Activities.** Children participate in music, art, drama, or other creative activities for at least three hours a week at home and elsewhere.
18. **Out-of-Home Activities.** Children spend one hour or more each week in extracurricular school activities or structured community programs.
19. **Religious Community.** The family attends religious programs or services for at least one hour per week.
20. **Positive, Supervised Time at Home.** Children spend most evenings and weekends at home with their parents in predictable, enjoyable routines.

INTERNAL ASSETS

Commitment to Learning

21. **Achievement Expectation and Motivation.** Children are motivated to do well in school and other activities.
22. **Children Are Engaged in Learning.** Children are responsive, attentive, and actively engaged in learning.
23. **Stimulating Activity and Homework.** Parents and teachers encourage children to explore and engage in stimulating activities. Children do homework when it's assigned.
24. **Enjoyment of Learning and Bonding to School.** Children enjoy learning and care about their school.
25. **Reading for Pleasure.** Children and an adult read together for at least 30 minutes a day. Children also enjoy reading or looking at books or magazines on their own.

Positive Values

26. **Family Values Caring.** Children are encouraged to help other people.
27. **Family Values Equality and Social Justice.** Children begin to show interest in making the community a better place.
28. **Family Values Integrity.** Children begin to act on their convictions and stand up for their beliefs.
29. **Family Values Honesty.** Children begin to value honesty and act accordingly.
30. **Family Values Responsibility.** Children begin to accept and take personal responsibility for age-appropriate tasks.
31. **Family Values Healthy Lifestyle.** Children begin to value good health habits and learn healthy sexual attitudes and beliefs as well as respect for others.

Social Competencies

32. **Planning and Decision Making.** Children begin to learn how to plan ahead and make choices at appropriate developmental levels.
33. **Interpersonal Skills.** Children interact with adults and children and can make friends. Children express and articulate feelings in appropriate ways and empathize with others.
34. **Cultural Competence.** Children know about and are comfortable with people of different cultural, racial, and/or ethnic backgrounds.
35. **Resistance Skills.** Children start developing the ability to resist negative peer pressure and dangerous situations.
36. **Peaceful Conflict Resolution.** Children try to resolve conflicts nonviolently.

Positive Identity

37. **Personal Power.** Children begin to feel they have control over things that happen to them. They begin to manage frustrations and challenges in ways that have positive results for themselves and others.
38. **Self-Esteem.** Children report having high self-esteem.
39. **Sense of Purpose.** Children report that their lives have purpose and actively engage their skills.
40. **Positive View of Personal Future.** Children are hopeful and positive about their personal future.

40 ASSETS MIDDLE AND HIGH SCHOOL KIDS NEED TO SUCCEED

(Ages 12 to 18 Years)

Search Institute has identified the following building blocks of healthy development that help young people grow up healthy, caring, and responsible.

CATEGORY	ASSET NAME AND DEFINITION
EXTERNAL ASSETS	
Support	1. **Family Support.** Kids feel loved and supported in their family.
	2. **Positive Family Communication.** Kids turn to their parents for advice and support. They have frequent, in-depth conversations with each other on a variety of topics. Parents are approachable and available when kids want to talk.
	3. **Other Adult Relationships.** Kids know other adults besides their parents they can turn to for advice and support. They have frequent, in-depth conversations with them. Ideally, three or more adults play this role in their lives.
	4. **Caring Neighborhood.** Kids feel that their neighbors support them, encourage them, and care about them.
	5. **Caring School Climate.** Kids feel that their school supports them, encourages them, and cares about them.
	6. **Parent Involvement in Schooling.** Parents are actively involved in helping kids succeed in school.
Empowerment	7. **Community Values Youth.** Kids perceive that adults in the community value young people.
	8. **Youth as Resources.** Kids are given useful roles in the community.
	9. **Service to Others.** Kids serve in the community one or more hours per week.
	10. **Safety.** Kids feel safe at home, at school, and in their neighborhood.
Boundaries and Expectations	11. **Family Boundaries.** Parents set clear rules and consequences for their kids' behavior. They monitor their children's whereabouts.
	12. **School Boundaries.** Schools set clear rules and consequences for student behavior.
	13. **Neighborhood Boundaries.** Neighbors take responsibility for monitoring young people's behavior.
	14. **Adult Role Models.** Parents and other adults model positive, responsible behavior.
	15. **Positive Peer Influence.** Children's best friends model responsible behavior. They are a good influence. They do well in school and stay away from risky behaviors such as alcohol and other drug use.
	16. **High Expectations.** Parents and teachers encourage kids to do well.
Constructive Use of Time	17. **Creative Activities.** Kids spend three or more hours per week in lessons or practice in music, theater, or other arts.
	18. **Youth Programs.** Kids spend three or more hours each week in sports, clubs, or organizations at school and/or in the community.
	19. **Religious Community.** Kids spend one or more hours each week in religious services or participating in spiritual activities.
	20. **Time at Home.** Kids go out with friends "with nothing special to do" two or fewer nights each week.
INTERNAL ASSETS	
Commitment to Learning	21. **Achievement Motivation.** Kids are motivated to do well in school.
	22. **School Engagement.** Kids are actively engaged in learning.
	23. **Homework.** Kids do at least one hour of homework every school day.
	24. **Bonding to School.** Kids care about their school.
	25. **Reading for Pleasure.** Kids read for pleasure three or more hours per week.
Positive Values	26. **Caring.** Kids place high value on helping other people.
	27. **Equality and Social Justice.** Kids place high value on promoting equality and reducing hunger and poverty.
	28. **Integrity.** Kids act on their convictions and stand up for their beliefs.
	29. **Honesty.** Kids tell the truth even when it's not easy.
	30. **Responsibility.** Kids accept and take personal responsibility for their actions and decisions.
	31. **Restraint.** Kids believe that it's important not to be sexually active or to use alcohol or other drugs.
Social Competencies	32. **Planning and Decision Making.** Kids know how to plan ahead and make choices.
	33. **Interpersonal Competence.** Kids have empathy, sensitivity, and friendship skills.
	34. **Cultural Competence.** Kids know and are comfortable with people of different cultural, racial, and/or ethnic backgrounds.
	35. **Resistance Skills.** Kids can resist negative peer pressure and avoid dangerous situations.
	36. **Peaceful Conflict Resolution.** Kids seek to resolve conflict nonviolently.
Positive Identity	37. **Personal Power.** Kids feel that they have control over many things that happen to them.
	38. **Self-Esteem.** Kids feel good about themselves.
	39. **Sense of Purpose.** Kids believe that their life has a purpose.
	40. **Positive View of Personal Future.** Kids are optimistic about their own future.

40 ASSETS FOR CHILDREN AND TEENS
(Birth to 18 Years)

How you build assets in young people depends on their age. Infants, toddlers, and preschoolers are more dependent on adults than are older children. For this reason, the asset definitions for young children put the responsibility for building both external and internal assets in the hands of parents and other caregiving adults. The chart on these two pages shows the progression of the assets across five age groups: infants, toddlers, preschoolers, elementary-age children, and teens.

EXTERNAL ASSETS				
Asset Type	Infants (Birth to 12 Months)	Toddlers (Ages 13 to 35 Months)	Preschoolers (Ages 3 to 5 Years)	Elementary-Age Children (Ages 6 to 11 Years)	Teens (Ages 12 to 18 Years)
Support	1. Family Support				
	2. Positive Family Communication				
	3. Other Adult Relationships				
	4. Caring Neighborhood				
	5. Caring Out-of-Home Climate			5. Caring School Climate	
	6. Parent Involvement in Out-of-Home Situations			6. Parent Involvement in Schooling	
Empowerment	7. Community Values Children				7. Community Values Youth
	8. Children Are Given Useful Roles				8. Youth as Resources
	9. Service to Others				
	10. Safety				
Boundaries and Expectations	11. Family Boundaries				
	12. Out-of-Home Boundaries			12. School Boundaries	
	13. Neighborhood Boundaries				
	14. Adult Role Models				
	15. Positive Peer Interactions and Influence				15. Positive Peer Interactions
	16. Appropriate Expectations for Growth				16. High Expectations
Constructive Use of Time	17. Creative Activities				
	18. Out-of-Home Activities				18. Youth Programs
	19. Religious Community				
	20. Positive, Supervised Time at Home				20. Time at Home

40 ASSETS FOR CHILDREN AND TEENS
(Birth to 18 Years)

INTERNAL ASSETS				
Asset Type	Infants (Birth to 12 Months)	Toddlers (Ages 13 to 35 Months)	Preschoolers (Ages 3 to 5 Years)	Elementary-Age Children (Ages 6 to 11 Years)	Teens (Ages 12 to 18 Years)
Commitment to Learning	21. Achievement Expectation and Motivation				21. Achievement Motivation
	22. Children Are Engaged in Learning			22. School Engagement	
	23. Stimulating Activity		23. Stimulating Activity and Homework		23. Homework
	24. Enjoyment of Learning and Bonding to School			24. Bonding to School	
	25. Reading for Pleasure				
Positive Values	26. Family Values Caring				26. Caring
	27. Family Values Equality and Social Justice				27. Equality and Social Justice
	28. Family Values Integrity				28. Integrity
	29. Family Values Honesty				29. Honesty
	30. Family Values Responsibility				30. Responsibility
	31. Family Values Healthy Lifestyle				31. Restraint
Social Competencies	32. Planning and Decision Making				
	33. Interpersonal Skills				33. Interpersonal Competence
	34. Cultural Competence				
	35. Resistance Skills				
	36. Peaceful Conflict Resolution				
Positive Identity	37. Personal Power				
	38. Self-Esteem				
	39. Sense of Purpose				
	40. Positive View of Personal Future				

WHAT TO EXPECT OF INFANTS

Because of the remarkable growth and change taking place in this year, experts break it down into three periods: birth to 3 months, 4 to 7 months, and 8 to 12 months. Even though babies master the same physical, cognitive, and social-emotional tasks, each infant does so on a very individual timetable. Here are some milestones during the first year of a child's life.

HOW INFANTS MOVE

- Newborns move their arms and legs and can lift their heads slightly and briefly when placed on their stomachs. Putting newborns on their stomachs lets them practice lifting their heads and developing their neck muscles. (However, place newborns on their stomachs for only short periods of time, and only during their waking hours. Experts currently believe that it's safer for babies to sleep on their backs. This ensures a clear flow of oxygen in order to prevent deaths due to SIDS— Sudden Infant Death Syndrome.)

- Infants typically begin to roll over at around the age of 4 to 5 months.

- Many infants begin to bear a little weight on their legs at around 5 to 6 months.

- Infants sit without support, starting typically at 6 to 7 months.

- Infants typically start standing while holding onto someone at around 8 to 9 months.

- Infants typically pull themselves to a standing position starting at around 9 to 10 months.

- Babies and toddlers begin walking by holding onto furniture or by holding both hands of another person and "toddling" from one stationary object to another. While some children start walking earlier, most babies don't begin walking until 13 to 15 months of age.

- As babies become mobile, give them constant supervision. Whenever they're around stairs, use baby gates to prevent accidents.

HOW INFANTS INTERACT WITH OTHERS

- Newborns spend a lot of time looking or staring intently at faces—often the faces of immediate family members.

- Infants begin to learn how to interact with others by watching. That's why it's so important for adults to model positive ways to communicate. For example, adults can look at each other as they talk and use facial expressions that clearly match their feelings.

- Many infants go through a friendly, social period at around 6 months. They smile, laugh out loud, squeal, coo, and babble. Encourage and delight in these social interactions. Your response invites an infant to interact more.

- Most infants go through a period known as *stranger anxiety*. This usually occurs at around 8 or 9 months, but it can happen earlier or later. Being wary of strangers typically doesn't last long. During this time, it's important to respect the infant's clinging, particularly if the infant cries for hours when separated from a primary caregiver. For example, when leaving an infant with a new caregiver, take time to chat with the new adult in a relaxed way. This will show the infant that you're comfortable with the caregiver. While you talk, hold the infant and offer reassurance: "I know you don't want me to go. You'll be safe here, and I'll be back." Though the baby won't understand your words, he or she will sense your confident tone and attitude.

WHAT TO EXPECT OF INFANTS

- Some infants may seem shy and may not appear to enjoy interacting with other people. That's okay. This may reflect the baby's individual temperament or indicate stranger anxiety. Help the infant feel comfortable by letting her or him get used to a new person or situation gradually.
- As infants become more verbal and mobile, encourage them to wave "bye-bye," blow kisses, clap, and say "hi." Teach these basic skills of interacting with others. Model other fundamentals, such as saying "please" and "thank you."

HOW INFANTS LEARN

- Babies grow, thrive, and learn when they are loved and cared for.
- One way infants learn is by interacting with others. Talk with them. Sing to them. Coo with them. Casual, stimulating exchanges teach infants how to interact and encourage healthy development.
- Some infants are highly sensitive to stimulation. These babies become upset when people talk loudly or when there's too much activity around. Other infants can become easily bored from too little stimulation. Infants learn best when they're calm, when they have a balance of stimulation and quiet, and when caregivers recognize and consider their individual differences.
- Don't focus on a baby's performance or push an infant to learn. Infants will learn on their own if adults create an environment that's warm, loving, stimulating, and relaxed. An infant comes "equipped" with an urge to develop and grow—it's up to adults to follow the child's lead.
- As infants become more mobile (typically at around 6 months), offer more stimulating things for them to do. Give them blocks, soft dolls, stuffed animals, and *large* household items such as mixing spoons, measuring cups, and pots and pans. Babies learn and explore by putting things in their mouths, so don't give them things with small parts that they could swallow.
- Early on, provide rattles and board books. Help infants shake a rattle and see how they can make a noise. Show infants pictures in a picture book. Read simple rhymes. Play a variety of music for the baby to listen to.
- Infants learn a great deal through play. See Handout #13, "Tips to Playing with Infants," for specific ideas.

BRINGING OUT THE BEST IN INFANTS

- Create an ideal environment. Infants blossom in stimulating environments that have interesting people and objects—such as books, rattles and other hand-held toys, baby gyms, and interactive toys with mirrors to look into and objects of different shapes and textures to hold, push, and pull on. Babies also thrive when they can sleep in soothing, quiet areas.
- Meet infants' needs immediately. As soon as they cry, find out what they need. Sometimes babies need food or a clean diaper. At other times they need sleep or activity. Some cries simply mean the baby needs to be held or talked to. Keep infants dry, fed, well rested, and involved in interesting things.
- Be *proactive* in relating to an infant—don't wait for the baby to cry or reach out to you. Talk with the baby. Sing. Dance. Listen to the child's coos and exclamations.
- Never push an infant to master a specific milestone. Follow the infant's lead, be encouraging, and enjoy growing and developing together.

TIPS FOR TALKING WITH INFANTS

Although all infants cry from the time they're born, babies learn how to talk by being exposed to language and watching and hearing how others communicate. According to the American Academy of Pediatrics, infants tend to notice pitch first, which is why talking with an infant in a soothing manner is so important. As infants grow, they begin experimenting with sounds. They also watch closely how others around them react—not only what others say, but also how they say it.

HOW INFANTS TALK

- Infants cry from birth. Crying is a major way infants communicate during the first 14 months of life.

- Infants coo, starting anywhere between the ages of 3 and 8 months.

- Infants laugh and squeal. Laughing out loud usually begins at around $3\frac{1}{2}$ months; squealing occurs about a month later.

- Infants babble, experimenting with sounds. Starting typically at around 6 months, they'll babble chains of sounds, such as "ba-ba-ba-ba."

- Infants make a wet "razzing" sound (which adults call "raspberries"), starting typically at around 6 to 7 months.

- Some infants say "dada" at 10 months, "mama" at 11 months, and sometimes one additional word by their first birthday. Most babies, however, won't speak in easily recognizable words until 14 months or later.

- Expect babies to gesture, point, and use a lot of nonverbal communication to express their needs. For example, babies will sometimes flap their arms when they're excited, begin to reach out to be picked up, and turn their head away to avoid an interaction they don't want to have.

HOW TO TALK TO INFANTS

- Talk *with* infants, not *at* them. Give babies time to express themselves in conversations. React to what they say. When babies coo, say, "Oh, you like that!" When babies cry, close their eyes, or turn their heads, say, "Okay, we'll stop that and take a break."

- Talk to an infant when you're alone together, even though the child won't say much in return. Tell the infant what's happening. For example, "I'm getting the squash and the spoon. Uff! This lid is tight. But I got it off. Hey, look how orange squash is. Here comes the first bite." As you talk, don't dominate conversation. Pause from time to time to let the baby respond. The response won't necessarily be words. For example, babies who like squash will often get excited when they see you sit down with a jar of squash for them.

- Ask questions, and pause for infants to answer. At first, you probably won't get much reaction out of an infant. But one day, a baby will surprise you. An infant may clap, grunt, gurgle, coo, or giggle in response to something you say. Encourage dialogue. Invite it.

- Begin to use the word "no" at around $7\frac{1}{2}$ to 10 months, suggests child development expert Burton White, Ph.D. Babies can begin to understand what the word means at around this age, though they usually won't obey it. Continue to repeat the word and use other methods to emphasize why you're saying "no." For example, if a baby is chewing on an electrical cord and won't stop when you say "no," remove the child from the area and offer a teething ring.

TIPS FOR TALKING WITH INFANTS

- Experiment with pitch. Babies tend to prefer high-pitched voices, which is why many people talk an octave or two higher when speaking with infants. See how the baby reacts when you speak as a soprano—or a bass.

- Imitate what babies say. Babies love it when someone burbles back at them when they burble. You can often create a game of mimicking the sounds an infant makes.

- Respect what infants' gestures and body language tell you. When babies close their eyes, become fussy, look away, or turn their heads, they're saying they've had enough. Respect this and, whenever possible, stop what you're doing.

- Read aloud. Infants love the sound of the human voice. Read board books, but don't limit your reading to children's materials. If you get excited about the NBA playoffs, read aloud the headlines of the sports page to your infant. If you're curious about a recipe, read aloud the ingredients that surprise you. Some parents even read aloud portions of a novel during middle-of-the-night feedings in order to keep themselves awake.

- Sing to infants. Experiment with sounds. Laugh. Have fun together.

TIPS FOR PLAYING WITH INFANTS

Playing with an infant is entertaining, but it's also more than that. Games can teach infants important skills, including how to interact with others. Playing often touches on many different aspects of development. No matter what type of play you're involved in together, be sensitive to how the baby reacts. Follow the child's enthusiasm. Stop when the infant gives you signals that she or he is finished or becoming tired or overstimulated.

TIPS FOR PLAYING WITH NEWBORNS UP TO THE AGE OF 3 MONTHS

- Find bright, high-contrast objects for newborns to look at. These may include a mobile, a large picture book, or certain newborn toys with high-contrast colors (especially black, white, and red).

- Hold newborns up to a mirror when they're alert. This is often fascinating to them.

- Play "distance" games: Put your face close to an infant's face. Hold it there for a few moments. Then move back. Do the same thing with objects.

- Give newborns interesting things to look at. Prop them up so they can see. Take them on walks where they have a full view of everything.

- Sing to babies. Dance with them. Be playful.

- Play with infants' hands and feet. "Pedal" their feet and say, "You're pretending to ride a bike!" Guide their hands to clap to the beat of music.

TIPS FOR PLAYING WITH 3- TO 7-MONTH-OLDS

- Provide rattles and other noisemakers for babies to shake. Infants can typically begin grasping and reaching for objects during this time frame. Even grasping an adult's finger can turn into a game for an infant.

- Create fun feeding games. As infants begin to eat solids, don't just shovel the food into their mouths. Play a games where they open their mouths to let the food in and shut them for a time before eating more.

- Give infants toys that are safe for their age. Toys will go into their mouths, so make sure the toys and toy parts aren't too small. Wash toys often. Never give a baby objects made of lead or other harmful substances.

- Provide toys that make sounds or toys that do something when the baby pushes, hits, or pokes them.

- Play "Where Did It Go?" Gently tease infants by briefly hiding a toy they like behind your back for a second or two, then bring it back into view. Say, "Where did it go? Oh—there it is!" Some infants think this is a fun game and like to watch a toy disappear and reappear.

- Play games of peek-a-boo. Put a clean diaper or towel over your head, take it off, and say "peek-a-boo!"

- Sing songs during dressing, diaper changes, and bathtime routines. Make up games for these times, such as "Where's Your Foot?" Look around, then grasp the infant's foot and say, "Here it is!" and kiss it.

TIPS FOR PLAYING WITH INFANTS

- Make games out of milestones that infants are practicing. For example, guide infants to do "sit-ups" at around 6 or 7 months of age, by gently pulling him or her up by the arms. (If the baby's head falls backward, the infant's not ready for this yet.) This game helps infants develop stronger neck muscles. It's also fun.

TIPS FOR PLAYING WITH 8- TO 12-MONTH-OLDS

- When an infant begins to enter the "drop-it" stage (in which they drop items and watch them fall), play "pick-up." Pick up the item and hand it to the infant. Keep doing this to turn it into a game.

- Play chanting, rhyming, or musical games such as "The Itsy Bitsy Spider," "This Little Piggy," "Pop Goes the Weasel," and "One, Two, Buckle My Shoe." A Mother Goose book is a great source of rhymes for this sort of game.

- Encourage babies to clap their hands to music—or to your singing. Guide a child in clapping games by putting your hands over the baby's. "Pat-a-Cake" is one of many fun clapping games.

- Hide objects for babies to find—although hide it while the baby is looking. For example, show a baby a toy and then put a scarf over it. Ask "Where did the toy go?" Babies usually laugh as they grab for the scarf.

- Find nesting toys, such as colored plastic barrels or cubes of diminishing sizes that fit inside one another. Babies at this age love putting objects into containers.

- Play dumping games. Babies love to dump out bowls, shoe boxes, plastic buckets, or anything else that holds things. Remember that babies usually put things in their mouths, so continue to be careful about small objects.

- Give babies playtimes that can give them a sense of motion, such as riding in a wagon or swinging in an infant swing. Some babies like to bounce on laps or dance in the arms of an adult.

WHAT TO EXPECT OF TODDLERS

Toddlers develop rapidly between 13 and 35 months. In fact, there is a lot of research on brain development focused on the first three years of life because of the long-term benefits to children who have an enriched, stimulating environment during this time. Many people have learned to think of the middle toddler years as "the terrible twos." While it's true that the resistance toddlers display is a critical part of their development, it's equally true that toddlers are going through many other remarkable developments as well. As often as they can be contrary, toddlers can be irresistible. Here are some milestones that occur during the second and third years of a child's life.

HOW TODDLERS MOVE

- Toddlerhood tends to begin when young children begin "toddling" as they walk.

- Somewhere between the ages of 16 and 21 months, toddlers begin to learn how to walk up and climb down stairs. Toddlers need constant supervision whenever they're around stairs. Continue using "baby gates" to prevent accidents around stairs.

- Expect toddlers to fall often and bump into everything. As they learn to walk, run, climb, and jump, they fall, flip over, and trip. Mastering these new motor skills will take a toddler some time.

- During toddlerhood, children are into everything: cupboards, drawers, boxes, closets, purses, toolboxes—anything they can figure out how to open. This means that the toddler years are busy years for toddlers' caregivers as well! Toddlers also love pushing buttons and switching on and off light switches that they can reach.

- Between the ages of 18 and 20 months, many toddlers learn how to run. Their running will be awkward.

HOW TODDLERS INTERACT WITH OTHERS

- Although toddlers embrace the world around them, many can also retreat to an adult's lap or arms at times. In fact, expect extremes in toddlers' behavior and feelings. One moment, they're crying and clingy. The next, they're dashing across the grass toward the street. (And, because they can't yet judge danger, they'll run out into the street. Toddlers need constant supervision when they're outdoors.)

- The "no-no-no" toddler years are what child development experts categorize as the years of negativism. Expect resistance. Respond to it patiently, but firmly. Follow through and act on what you say. For example, if a toddler keeps trying to eat the cat's food, say "no" and then remove the cat bowl.

- Most toddlers appear to be self-centered in their behavior. "Mine" is the second most common word in a toddler's vocabulary (the first is "no"). Instinctively, they'll grab, pull, and run off with things that belong to other people. The "mine" stage is the toddler's first understanding of ownership. This is a good time to begin teaching the concept of sharing.

- Toddlers don't know how to act in what adults consider to be socially acceptable ways. They need to observe people around them acting courteously and respectfully. They also need many opportunities to interact with adults, siblings, and other toddlers. Although most of these interactions will not be smooth, they're an important training ground for toddlers. It's through experimenting (and often struggling) with getting along with others that toddlers begin to learn acceptable ways to act.

WHAT TO EXPECT OF TODDLERS

HOW TODDLERS LEARN

- Toddlers are naturally curious, but curiosity needs to be cultivated. When toddlers ask questions, answer them (even if they asked the same question 50 times). Get excited about what toddlers squeal about. Point out things that interest you, too.

- Encourage toddlers to experiment. Toddlers will learn a great deal just by playing in a sandbox, but you can also encourage learning by asking questions. "What if you pour the sand out of the bucket? What if you hold the sand and open up your fingers? What if you make a big sand hill and then sit on it?"

- Toddlers learn from being exposed to new situations. Take a toddler to the park to swing and slide. There are many other things toddlers can do and learn from, including planting seeds, pushing an elevator button, scribbling on paper, and ringing a doorbell.

- Toddlers love to read with adults, and one of the best ways to help toddlers learn is through books. Have lots of books around. Toddlers will often spend time looking at the pictures. They like to have you read to them, and they also like to look at books themselves.

BRINGING OUT THE BEST IN TODDLERS

- Create an exciting environment. Take toddlers to new places (such as zoos, parks, and pet shops), but don't expect them to have a long attention span. Play with toddlers in a variety of different areas. Go outside. Stay inside. Play in the kitchen. Play in the bedroom.

- Just as toddlers learn from asking questions, they can learn when you ask questions, too. Ask questions often. When reading, point to different animals and ask, "What's that?" When walking with a toddlers, ask, "What do you see?"

- Spend time with toddlers. Just hang out and see what they want to do. Follow their agenda.

- Accentuate what's wonderful about toddlers. They're curious. They're funny. They're dramatic. Focus on the positive while setting boundaries to keep them safe and to begin teaching them how to behave in many different situations (such as inside, outside, with adults, with children, with pets, and so on).

- Celebrate toddlers' accomplishments. When they can climb the stairs, applaud them. When they throw the ball for the first time, make a big deal about it.

TIPS FOR TALKING WITH TODDLERS

Toddlers gradually learn to articulate their needs and communicate more easily with adults through simple language. Although young toddlers typically have only a few words at their command, they communicate a lot by combining a word with gestures, sounds, and body language. As they get older, toddlers will begin to string words together in sentences.

HOW TODDLERS TALK

Like infants, toddlers have their own language that includes a mixture of words, sounds, actions, and facial expressions. Keep in mind that all these forms of communication make up a toddler's "talk."

- Crying is still a major way young toddlers talk, although many quickly learn other ways to communicate their needs. For examples, toddlers will tug on your clothes to get your attention.

- Nonverbal communication and gestures often make up most of a toddler's communication skills at first. Toddlers will point to things they want. They'll use a lot of facial expressions to show their likes and dislikes.

- Expect toddlers to "act" as a way of communicating. For example, some toddlers who get excited will jump up and down. Some will fall to the floor and cover their heads with their hands when they feel hurt. An angry toddler can begin running in circles and screaming. Toddlers will have tantrums when they become upset. Although their actions are a dramatic way to "talk," toddlers need adults around them to take what they have to say seriously and to help them learn more appropriate ways to communicate.

- Some toddlers learn words faster than others. According to child development experts, it's normal by the age of 2 for a toddler to have a vocabulary of anywhere from 24 to 400 words. Early talking is not a sign of high intelligence, just as late talking isn't a sign of low intelligence. All children develop according to their own tempo and learning style.

HOW TO TALK TO TODDLERS

- An important part of talking with toddlers is labeling objects. Most toddlers will ask, "Wha dat?" ("What's that?") over and over, as a way of learning labels. Toddlers won't learn the labels the first, second, or even third time they hear them, so keep answering their questions by naming the object. By about 18 months, many toddlers can name six body parts. Naming animals comes later. Learning colors by name comes later still.

- Listen to toddlers. Many love to talk, and parents and caregivers affectionately call them "chatterboxes." Even if you don't completely understand what toddlers are saying, look at them, listen, and give them the respect they deserve as they talk. Sometimes toddlers speak something called *mother tongue*—they string many words and nonwords together with lots of intonation changes similar to those that all conversations have. Often a child's primary caregivers can understand every "word." People who don't know the toddler well won't understand, but they can recognize by the elaborate string of sounds that the toddler is saying something very important.

- Talk like an adult. Toddlers' words often sound adorable, and it's tempting to mimic the words, but don't. Calmly use the correct word in your response. For example, when a toddler says, "Me eat sketti," reply in a friendly tone, "Yes, you're eating spaghetti." Toddlers need to hear correct speech so they can gradually master it.

TIPS FOR TALKING WITH TODDLERS

- Let some "friendly" family labels stick. For example, "Grandpa" and "Grandma" are typically difficult for a toddler to say. It's okay if the child creates other labels for grandparents. Some toddlers call their grandma "Nana," "Oma," or "Gammy." Some call their grandpa "Bapa," "Opa," or "Gampa." One toddler thought his grandma was named "Huh" because his grandpa always said "Huh?" whenever she spoke to the grandfather. As long as the people being addressed are comfortable with their new names, allow toddlers to use them. Over time these names are often affectionate reminders of the relationships between young children and other family members.

- Be a translator. Although toddlers often speak in ways that are hard for others to understand, if *you* know what the toddler is saying, rephrase it for the listener. This makes it easier for others who don't spend much time with the toddler to learn the child's language.

- Encourage speech, don't discourage it. Along with the labels they're learning, toddlers are also learning the many rules of language, such as syntax, grammar, and pronunciation. This level of sophistication will take years for a child to master. Don't criticize or continually correct toddlers' errors. These errors are a normal part of language development. By listening, replying with correct words and phrasing, and conversing in a friendly way, you can help make learning language fun for toddlers.

TIPS FOR PLAYING WITH TODDLERS

One of the best ways to spend time with a toddler is through play. Contrary to what our competitive, time-focused society sometimes seems to suggest, playing is not a waste of time. Play is critical for a all children's growth. In fact, it's the primary way toddlers and other young children learn. Nothing can compete with the valuable time toddlers spend playing with an adult, with another child, or on their own with age-appropriate playthings.

TIPS FOR PLAYING WITH 13- TO 18-MONTH-OLDS

- Beach balls are a great toy for this age group, since they're lightweight and interesting to carry. Rolling a ball back and forth (and doing this with balls of different sizes) is also stimulating to a young toddler.

- Engage young toddlers in pretending. Pretend to eat a sandwich and then rub your belly and lick your lips. Pretend to drink juice from an empty cup and offer the cup to the toddler to take a pretend drink. Any pretend play that pertains to a toddler's world (eating, drinking, washing, and other daily routines) will often be a big hit.

- When you're out of ideas for keeping a toddler entertained, try some water play. Toddlers love to splash, drop things in water, and see what things float. (Keep in mind that a toddler playing with water—whether in a sink, a tub, inflatable swimming pool, a water table, or even a large bowl or sprinkler—needs constant supervision.)

- Make reading fun. Get books with animals in them. Together make the different sounds of the animals you see on the page. You can also read books about machines and make the noises the bull-dozers, airplanes, and vacuum cleaners make.

- One of the best ways to capture the attention of a 14- to 15-month-old is with a Ping-Pong ball on a hardwood floor, suggests child development expert Burton White, Ph.D. Toddlers can spend lots of time giggling and chasing a bouncing Ping-Pong ball.

- Use toddler-safe household items for play. Create a pile of empty film containers or empty thread spools and give a toddler a box or plastic container. Together, put the items in. Then let the toddler dump them out and put them back in again.

TIPS FOR PLAYING WITH 19- TO 35-MONTH-OLDS

- You can have a lot of fun playing stacking games with toddlers at this age. Although toddlers won't be able to stack things high (six items is usually the maximum for a toddler), they like to help with the stacking, and they love pushing over stacks that you make.

- Do puzzles together. Wooden puzzles (particularly the ones with knobs on the pieces) delight many older toddlers.

- Play dressing games with dolls and stuffed animals. Toddlers love to put clothes and hats on different animals (as long as the clothes aren't too tight). Some toddlers enjoy trying on different clothes themselves.

- Make daily routines a game. Bathtime can be a playtime, as can getting dressed and undressed. Some toddlers enjoy having a simple chasing game before they get undressed for a bath. (They'll run in and out of different rooms as the adult slowly chases them. Don't be too quick to catch them, but when at last you do, scoop the toddler up and say, "I got you!")

TIPS FOR PLAYING WITH TODDLERS

- Engage toddlers in pretend play. Although toddlers aren't ready for imaginative worlds, they love to act in the ways of the world they know. Pretend to water plants. Pretend to sweep the floor. Pretend to hammer nails to hang a picture or turn a screwdriver to fix a loose knob on a cupboard. Pretend to cook a meal and eat it.

- Sometimes paper can keep you and a toddler busy for a long time. Recycle paper by giving it to toddlers to draw on. When both sides of the page are full, let toddlers crumple, rip, or find another way to use the paper.

- Make learning a game. Go to the zoo or visit a farm. Ask toddlers which animals they know by name. Ask them which they know by sound. Teach toddlers other names and other sounds. Or go to a children's museum where there are hands-on exhibits for busy toddlers.

- Make book reading a theatrical experience for toddlers. Read dramatically. Change the voice for each character. Use a variety of facial expressions. Experiment with other ways to make reading fun and interesting to a toddler.

- When all else fails, grab a ball. Play different games with a ball. Toddlers are learning to kick and to throw. They can have a blast carrying a ball and running away from you. Toddlers also enjoy it when you roll a ball in their direction and they have to chase it to get it. Experiment with different, simple games using a ball.

WHAT TO EXPECT OF PRESCHOOLERS

The magic years. That's how the American Academy of Pediatrics characterizes the preschool years. Fantasy, imaginary play, and vivid storytelling make up the world of preschoolers, but children at this age are also mastering more and more skills while learning how to express themselves.

HOW PRESCHOOLERS MOVE

- Constant motion can describe the preschool years. Preschoolers don't walk, they run. They don't move through a room, they fly. Don't be surprised if you suddenly see a preschooler drop to the floor and begin slithering like a snake.

- As preschoolers grow, they become more agile at walking, running, jumping, going up and down stairs, and moving forward and backward.

- Expect preschoolers to be inconsistent with certain movements. A preschooler may stand on one foot easily one day, and have trouble the next. The same can be true of standing on tiptoes or getting up from a squatting position without falling over.

- Expect falls and accidents. While preschoolers continue to become more agile, they're still developing the judgment and self-control. Bumps and bruises are common.

- Preschoolers are learning to be more and more coordinated in using a ball. They kick, throw, and play simple catch. Most of their movement, however, is forward.

- Toward the end of the preschool years, many children will be able to hop, somersault, swing, and climb. Some can even skip.

HOW PRESCHOOLERS INTERACT WITH OTHERS

- By the preschool years, children begin to play with each other rather than side by side. Still, they don't play with other children consistently. They may play together for a few minutes and then wander off and play alone for awhile before coming back to play with a child.

- Through the preschool years, children begin to gravitate toward certain children more than others. By age 4 or 5, some preschoolers even have a "best friend."

- Expect preschoolers to physically act out their feelings at times, by hitting when they get angry or throwing something on the floor and crying. Tell preschoolers that hitting isn't okay. Encourage preschoolers to use their words instead of actions to express their feelings. If necessary, separate preschoolers when someone won't stop hitting or kicking.

- As preschoolers learn more words and have more command over language, they also learn the power of words. They can become bossy and will even boss around adults. This is a normal part of development.

- Preschoolers are experiencing complex feelings and complicated interactions. In doing this, they'll misbehave at times. Help preschoolers to make the distinction between themselves and their inappropriate actions—to separate the deed from the doer. Be clear and consistent with consequences for inappropriate behavior, but also be reassuring to children so they don't think they're "bad." For example, if a child loses her temper and shouts at you, you might reply, "I know you're angry with me. But it's not okay to yell. Let's talk quietly about this." This tells the child that her feelings are acceptable, but that her behavior isn't.

WHAT TO EXPECT OF PRESCHOOLERS

- Preschoolers can go in and out of fantasy and reality. They love to make believe. Follow their lead in this. For example, as you're shopping for groceries, a preschooler may stand behind a floor display and say, "I'm hiding. Let's play hide-and-seek." Count to 10 and play. Then go back to shopping.

HOW PRESCHOOLERS LEARN

- Preschoolers are learning more and more labels for the things in their world. During the preschool years, they're learning colors, some numbers, and some letters of the alphabet. Make this learning fun, using real-life items or pictures in books. But don't push children to master these skills.

- The preschool years should focus on learning to socialize. Give preschoolers opportunities to play with other children and to be with adults. This allows them to practice communicating and negotiating with others.

- Expect a constant string of questions. "Why?" questions often dominate a preschooler's thinking. Take these questions seriously. Be honest if you don't know the answer; try to find the information together.

- Preschoolers are learning the difference between "same" and "different." Create games and learning opportunities to encourage this learning. For example, play color games in which preschoolers name things that are red (such as strawberries, cardinals, and wagons) and things that are blue (such as blueberries, blue jays, and the sky).

- With preschoolers, a good deal of learning happens by examining and doing things with their fingers and hands. Give children puzzles to put together, paper to color and draw on, large beads to string, blocks to build with. Introduce blunt-tipped scissors made for preschoolers' hands, and expect that it will take children a number of years to master the ability to cut.

- Preschoolers slowly begin to comprehend the concept of time. The most effective way to teach this concept is by setting predictable routines. This helps preschoolers know what to expect when and what happens in the morning, the afternoon, the evening, today, yesterday, and tomorrow.

BRINGING OUT THE BEST IN PRESCHOOLERS

- Create an interesting environment. Give preschoolers a variety of materials to experiment with. For example, it's fun to paint with a brush, but it's also an interesting challenge to blow wet paint through a straw onto a sheet of paper or to "finger paint" with feet as well as hands.

- Be there. Although preschoolers are learning to be more independent, they still need time with caring adults.

- Create opportunities for imagination to develop. For example, collect adult-size dress-up clothes and shoes. Be sure to collect both men's and women's clothes. Ask for donations from family members, friends, and neighbors. Put the clothes in a large box for preschoolers to have available whenever they want to dress up.

- Be patient. Preschoolers still can act in highly emotional ways. Be calm in the way you react. Continue to teach appropriate ways for children to express their feelings.

TIPS FOR TALKING WITH PRESCHOOLERS

Between the years of 3 and 5, children rapidly increase their vocabulary. If you were to put a 3-year-old next to a 4-year-old and a 5-year-old, you'd be likely to hear an amazing difference in language ability among the children. In many ways, the speed of language acquisition for preschoolers is like a car going from zero to 60 mph.

HOW PRESCHOOLERS TALK

- While 3-year-olds have limited vocabularies (about 300 words), it's typical that the number of words they use will jump to 1,500 by age 4 and to 2,500 by age 5, says the American Academy of Pediatrics.

- Expect preschoolers to mispronounce a lot of words. For example, many preschoolers use a "w" instead of an "r," saying "wat" and "wed" instead of "rat" and "red." They will mispronounce other words as well.

- Preschoolers mimic the language they hear the adults around them speak. If you're hearing a lot of inappropriate language, pay attention to where preschoolers are picking up these words. Be clear that swearing is unacceptable. Say, "We don't talk that way."

- According to the American Academy of Pediatrics, one in 20 children stutters during the preschool years. Stuttering is more common for boys than girls. Most children outgrow stuttering.

- Some preschoolers learn words and how to put together sentences faster than others. Expect preschoolers to vary widely in their language acquisition skills. This is normal.

HOW TO TALK TO PRESCHOOLERS

- Draw attention to words pronounced correctly. Affirm the new words preschoolers learn. Focus on what the child is learning, not on what the child still hasn't mastered. For example, a child might say, "I catched that ball extremely good!" and you might reply, "Wow, what a great word you've learned—*extremely*. Can you tell me more about when you caught the ball?"

- Encourage preschoolers to use manners. Older preschoolers can become bossy, saying, "Come here *now*." Many preschoolers who want to talk interrupt adults and tell them to "stop talking." Explain that it's not okay to interrupt. Teach children to wait to speak, and to make a request using "please" rather than give an order. Be sure to model the same kind of courtesy.

- Listen to preschoolers, but also teach them how to listen to others. Emphasize the concepts of *taking turns* with talking and *listening* when others speak.

- Children quickly pick up on the fact that certain words have shock value and power. When they swear or use "bathroom language," be clear that those words are inappropriate. Teach children other alternatives for expressing feelings, getting attention, or being silly.

- If a child frequently stutters, encourage the child (and others around the child) to slow down. Stress makes stuttering worse. Do your best not to focus on stuttering. Just listen to what the child is saying and be respectful. If the stuttering becomes severe, talk to a pediatrician about your concerns.

- Read stories to preschoolers. Many are eager to listen to stories, and their attention spans are getting longer. Preschoolers are cultivating listening skills when others read books aloud.

TIPS FOR TALKING WITH PRESCHOOLERS

- Keep instructions to preschoolers simple. They'll miss some or all of what you say if you begin giving detailed explanations. Although preschoolers' talk can be impressive, it's easy to overestimate what they actually understand.

- Set clear boundaries about what's appropriate to say to others. Be consistent in upholding the boundaries. For example, preschoolers often can use harsh words, such as "I hate you" or "Go home!" Teach children acceptable ways to express their feelings and interact with other people. For example, teach preschoolers to articulate specifically what's happening and how they feel about it: "Stop taking my truck. That makes me mad."

- Listen to preschoolers' stories. Most children at this age can spin great tales. Ask a preschooler to tell you a story, and you may find yourself captivated by an incredible storyteller.

TIPS FOR PLAYING WITH PRESCHOOLERS

From extravagant clashes with dragons to flying through the air like Peter Pan, playing with a preschooler is always an adventure. Imaginary play is big with this age group, but so is reality. Playing ball outside or dressing up like a police officer can be equally enjoyable for children at this age.

TIPS FOR PLAYING WITH 3- TO 5-YEAR-OLDS

- Find out what preschoolers like to do. Children are all different. Some love dinosaurs. Others aren't interested in dinosaurs at all. Follow preschoolers' lead and build on their interests.

- Take preschoolers to places they'll find interesting. If a preschooler gets excited about digging up rocks in the backyard, go to a natural history museum, take a walk along a rocky path or shoreline, or see if you can visit a stone quarry. If a preschooler wants to be a ballet dancer, go to a dance studio or attend a recital for children. Keep such outings geared to the child's attention span.

- Also introduce preschoolers to new toys and new ways to play. Just as it's important to follow children's interests, it's equally worthwhile to keep exposing them to new types of play.

- Give preschoolers a vehicle to ride. Tricycles are a big hit with this age group. Walk alongside of them as they ride.

- Emphasize the arts. Most preschoolers love to sing, dance, act, paint, or draw. Some adults like things to be orderly, but loosening up and encouraging a little sloppiness gives children freedom to explore their artistic creativity.

- Join in preschoolers' imaginary play. If a child says you're the bad guy and starts running off, pretend to be that bad guy and try to catch the child. Let the preschooler chase *you* and put imaginary handcuffs on you.

- Create tunnels, hideaways, and other places for preschoolers to crawl into and play. (Make sure these are safe.) A blanket draped over a couple of chairs can become a tent. An appliance box can become a space ship.

- Enjoy outdoor activities on a regular basis with preschoolers. Play ball. Go to the park. Run races. Play hopping, jumping, skipping, and bouncing games.

- Be dramatic in your reading. You might even dress up as a character and be outlandish.

- Play singing games, such as "Ring Around the Rosy" and "The Itsy Bitsy Spider."

- Transform everyday items into toys. For example, a small box can be a bone for a dog. An empty egg carton can be a ship for 12 passengers.

- Become part of a preschooler's drama. Children at this age love to give puppet shows and to act in a theatrical performance. Either join in with the drama or be the enthusiastic audience.

- Build, build, build. With a preschooler, build with sand, mud, water, and dirt. Create towers out of boxes or blocks. Stack plastic containers. You don't need to buy items for building. Just start emptying some of those kitchen cupboards.

- Emphasize humor. Read books that are a humorous. Tell simple jokes. Ask preschoolers to tell you jokes. Preschoolers also like books and stories with funny sounds and made-up words, such as those found in Dr. Seuss books.

- Not sure what to play with a preschooler? Don't come with an agenda. Just show up and ask what the child would like to play. The ideas will be endless.

WHAT TO EXPECT OF ELEMENTARY-AGE CHILDREN

As children head off to school, their world expands. Families are still important, but children are beginning to spend more time with friends, homework, activities, and school events. At the same time children are developing social skills, their problem-solving, reasoning, and logical-thinking skills are emerging and growing.

HOW ELEMENTARY-AGE CHILDREN MOVE

- Between the ages of 6 and 11, children gradually master certain skills that have to do with eye-hand coordination. For example, they are becoming more adept at throwing a ball. Catching a ball, however, may be a different matter. While many 10-year-olds are capable of catching a fly ball, most 6- and 7-year-olds are probably not.

- It's normal for children to have an abundance of energy. It's also typical for them to be interested in watching a lot of television, which in turn can lead them to become less active. Encourage a balance of activity that gets children moving but also allows some downtime. There are many activities besides television and computer games that children will enjoy. For example, after outside play, a child may like to work on an art project, read, build a model, spend time with trucks or dolls, or play a board game.

- Puberty often begins during the elementary-age years. According to the American Academy of Pediatrics, it's not uncommon for girls to show the first outward signs of puberty at age 9 or 10, with some boys showing signs about a year or 18 months later. There is a good deal of individual variation, however, in both the timing and pace of puberty. For example, one 10-year-old girl may have begun to develop breasts and even started menstruating while another may not yet show any signs of pubertal development. One 11-year-old boy may experience nighttime ejaculation (wet dreams) while another does not.

- There is a great deal of individual variation in children's activity levels. Some children are more active than others. Encourage their passion for high-energy (or quiet) activity, but also create opportunities for them to stretch. Athletic children will benefit from learning how to do crafts. Children who constantly read benefit from getting outdoors to play.

- Some children push their limits and then seem to drop from exhaustion. During the elementary years, children can slowly begin to learn how to monitor their energy levels. Guide children to develop self-awareness of both feelings (crankiness, overexcitement, restlessness) and body signals (hunger, sleepiness, aches and pains) that can tell them they're overdoing, in need of rest, or ready for more physical activity.

HOW ELEMENTARY-AGE CHILDREN INTERACT WITH OTHERS

- Children at this age are learning how to cooperate in groups, play by the rules of a game, and play with other children. Children still need help in developing socially acceptable behavior, however.

- Children in the middle-elementary years, typically starting at around 8 or 9, may begin to be more competitive in their play. Team sports are one kind of competitive activity that often interest elementary-age children and are provide an opportunity to develop social skills and master physical skills.

- Boys may tend to play exclusively with boys, and girls exclusively with girls. Expect children to play mainly with children of the same sex, but don't discourage girl-boy friendships.

WHAT TO EXPECT OF ELEMENTARY-AGE CHILDREN

- Children typically develop close friendships during the elementary-school years. Many children have a best friend. Some children may even rank their friends in hierarchical order or categorize friends according to what they like to do together.

- Some children start secret clubs. They're interested in knowing how to belong, who to include, and what it means to be excluded. While clubs can be fun and can help children form close ties, be alert to a situation where a child may be feeling left out. Help children find ways to include others or to enjoy their exclusive club time when other kids aren't around.

- Parents are very important to elementary-age children—even though kids may sometimes say that their friends are more so. Children are aware of the time their parents spend together with them. As their social lives get busier, elementary-age children still need to have regular meals, activities, and "hanging out" time with their family. Family together-time is important for children of all ages.

HOW ELEMENTARY-AGE CHILDREN LEARN

- Children at this age learn best through active participation. Although they're becoming more able to sit and work at a desk, many children tend to learn more readily when they can become involved in a hands-on way. Because there is a good deal of individual variation in children's ability to sit still and do "seatwork," varying their activity works well. Allow for children to learn by hearing, writing, drawing, listening, touching, interacting, and doing. For example, to learn about plants and trees, children might collect and compare leaves, place a stalk of celery in blue-tinted water to see how plants absorb moisture, draw diagrams of a tree's trunk or branches, create a poster depicting how leaves and seeds emerge and change throughout the year, listen to music or poetry about the outdoor world, and plant a bush or seedling and care for it as it grows.

- This is the age of collections. Children learn a lot by collecting baseball cards, rocks, and stamps. Collecting gives children the opportunity to organize, categorize, and sort in addition to information they pick up about the topic of their collection.

- Children's thinking evolves around the present, not the distant future. They're interested in learning about what's around them and affecting them *now*. Although their goals tend to be immediate, elementary-age children can begin to learn to put off their some wants or desires for something in the future—for example, by saving money for something special.

- One of the major learning tasks for this age group is the development of the ability to complete a project from start to finish. Most children are naturally used to doing small, easy tasks. They may struggle with things that take more time or have more complicated steps. Kids will need adult assistance with planning such tasks.

- Children still have a relatively short attention span and may be easily distracted. This changes gradually over the span of years.

- Children at this age are generally eager to learn. The elementary years are a critical time in developing curiosity and motivation. Children who lose interest in learning at this age may not develop important academic skills they'll need later.

WHAT TO EXPECT OF ELEMENTARY-AGE CHILDREN

- Children learn best in environments that are full of interesting materials and meaningful activities. These things needn't be expensive. Craft materials like paper, markers, paints, and clay are available in discount stores. Libraries have computers children can use as well as books, tapes, and CDs they can borrow. Tag sales are a great place to purchase playthings such as Legos, dolls and doll clothes, games, action figures, puzzles, and sports equipment.

BRINGING OUT THE BEST IN ELEMENTARY-AGE CHILDREN

- Take seriously how children are growing and developing during this age period. It's often easy to think of these years as "the quiet years" that are sandwiched between preschool and puberty. Although children elementary-age can be easy to get along with, independent, and not as much "work" as younger or older children, they still need and thrive on attention from parents and teachers. They need caring adults to teach them skills, support and empower them, and challenge them in stimulating ways.

- Expose children to new experiences. Don't be too quick to get them focused exclusively on one thing, such as gymnastics, soccer, or skating. Introduce them to museums (most have free family days), parks, cultural fairs, and butterfly farms. Take them to plays, music performances, and community events. Gather together with other families for meals and group activities.

- Listen to children. They have interesting things to say and lots of great ideas. Give their stories and suggestions your full attention. Take time for thoughtful conversations.

- Expect children to act inconsistently and inappropriately at times. Continue to be clear about setting and enforcing boundaries.

- Have fun together. Run races. Go bike riding. Exchange riddles. See who has the silliest laugh. Simple shared pleasures create lasting memories and teach children ways that families and friends can stay connected.

TIPS FOR TALKING WITH ELEMENTARY-AGE CHILDREN

School-age children are interesting to talk to. They're soaking up information and they love to share what they're learning. Kids come up with many creative ideas and have a refreshing perspective on many subjects and issues.

HOW ELEMENTARY-AGE CHILDREN TALK

- The way children communicate depends a lot on individual personality. Some children are very open and talkative. Others are more reserved and private. Be respectful of each child's style, but teach children effective ways to communicate. For example, you may need to guide a talkative child to speak more slowly or not to interrupt. You may need to encourage a quieter child to be assertive when necessary.

- Elementary-age children still often "act out" what they're trying to say. When they slam doors or scowl, they're usually not purposely misbehaving—they're expressing things in a way that comes more naturally than words. It takes time to develop the maturity to state feelings clearly and respectfully. This doesn't mean adults should accept door slamming or chair kicking. Guide children to communicate through words. You might say, "I can see how upset you are, but slamming the door isn't the way to tell me. Please take a breath and try to calm down so we can talk about it."

- Children go through periods when they use "bathroom" language. They're intrigued with bodily functions. Don't be alarmed at hearing some vulgar language, but do be clear about what's acceptable and what's not.

- Expect children to begin setting boundaries around talking. For example, they may say, "There's nothing to talk about" even when others around them *do* think there's something that needs to be discussed. Some children need time to think through an experience before talking about it. You may also notice children working out feelings and experiences through play. For example, you may see children role-playing harsh words spoken to them by a coach or interactions in which one child bullies another. Be clear that aggressive play actions directed toward another person or oneself is never appropriate. Teach children to use words instead of actions to express anger and frustration.

- Children often communicate in similar ways as the people around them. If they spend a lot of time with adults who don't share feelings, they tend not to share them either. If they hang out with people who talk easily about things, they tend to do the same.

HOW TO TALK TO ELEMENTARY-AGE CHILDREN

- Pay attention to what they have to say. Listen. Ask questions. Give children your full attention.

- Work to understand what the child is saying rather than jump in to express your viewpoint. Many children don't articulate their thoughts clearly at first. Help them express themselves more clearly by listening, summarizing, and repeating back what you think children are trying to say.

- With elementary-age children, it's easy to get into a pattern of arguing over a wide variety of things. Avoid too many power struggles. It's usually more fruitful to listen to what children have to say and yet be firm about values and principles (such as honesty and caring) than about the type of shirt a child wants to wear. Give in sometimes about issues that are less important. This is what is meant when people say, "Choose your battles."

TIPS FOR TALKING WITH ELEMENTARY-AGE CHILDREN

- Listen closely to a child's emotional tone when he or she talks. Often the unspoken, underlying message is what the child is really trying to tell you. Point out these messages and help interpret their feelings. For example, "You seem rather sad as you talk about this. What's got you feeling sad?"

- Never put down a child. Use "I-messages" and avoid "you-messages." For example, after a child has pushed his younger brother down, an effective I-message would be: "I was so scared when Paul hit his head! And I get really mad when I see someone bigger hurting someone smaller." Notice how much more constructive an I-message is than a you-message like this would be: "You idiot! Why did you push your brother like that! You know better than that." You-messages usually escalate disagreements, because the child feels accused and so fights back. Expressing your feelings in a respectful way shows children a mature and helpful way to handle difficult situations.

- Watch the timing of conversations. For example, some children don't want to talk the minute they come home from school. They may want a chance to unwind first. Find a time when both you and the child can focus on the conversation.

- Tell children about adult matters that will affect them, but don't burden them with adult descriptions and problems. For example, if parents are thinking about getting a divorce, they should wait to talk about this with the child once a decision has been made—not before. It's also important to anticipate children's concerns and to be prepared to answer them honestly, but without worrying children. Children don't cope well with adult indecision, especially if they don't know what it means for them. Children also may become very anxious about how an adult issue such as divorce or the loss of a job may affect them. Do your best to explain things matter of factly. Reassure children that they will still be safe and cared for, while guarding yourself from making unrealistic promises that you can't keep.

- Find ways to connect with children about things they're doing outside of school. Ask about their favorite NBA team, what they're doing on Saturday, or who their best friend is and why. Too many children are only asked, "How's school this year. Do you like it?" Ask questions that are specific and that tie in to a child's interest.

TIPS FOR PLAYING WITH ELEMENTARY-AGE CHILDREN

As children go to school, play continues to be an important part of their development. While it's true that younger children tend to gravitate toward different types of play than older children, the type of play that elementary-age children enjoy doing also begins to vary based on their individual interests as well as their age.

TIPS FOR PLAYING WITH 6- TO 11-YEAR-OLDS

- Find out what children like to play. Some like quieter, indoor activities (such as drawing or painting) while others like more activity (such as being the first ones out the door with a ball). Ask if you can join in.

- Children with high energy like to do anything where they can "tear around." Games such as tag and hide-and-seek are popular.

- You may notice some gender differences in what boys and girls play with during this age period. These differences may often be along fairly stereotypical gender roles. Many girls enjoy dressing and undressing dolls, and they may also be interested in accessories for dolls, such as suitcases, furniture, cribs, and so on. Boys may like playing with action figures, and they may also love magic tricks, mixing up contents in chemistry sets to make magic potions, and using tools to build things such as erector sets and model cars. However, it is very important that both boys and girls be encouraged to develop what interests them rather than choosing something because it's what "girls do" or what "boys do."

- Follow children's lead in their play. Ask them what they enjoy doing and let them choose. Pay close attention to children's skill level in play and what makes them excited versus what frustrates them. Adjust your playing so that you and the child are more equally matched. If you're feeling super-competitive, restrain yourself and find another adult to compete with later.

- Board games are a big hit with this age group. From dominoes to cards to checkers, children love to play games. Make the play fun and focus on what's going well for the child. Sometimes it's good to lose on purpose, but not all the time. Children need to learn that they won't always win, and it's best that they learn this "life lesson" in a supportive environment. Don't be surprised if a younger child changes the rules in the middle of the game, cheats in order to win, or sulks after losing. Remind the child that cheating is dishonest; encourage a sporting attitude. Monitor how children react to winning and losing and talk through your concerns about their behavior. Also point out when you're happy with how they're acting.

- Tie playing to learning. Some children think it's fun to do math problems. Others have a blast pretending to be the referee of a game. Still others will ask you to be the student while they're the teacher.

- Children enjoy watching television, and they have their favorite shows. Watch one of their favorites with them. Afterward, talk about what you liked about it. Ask questions to find out why the child liked it.

- Develop more challenging play. For example, children often like to have playoffs and championship games where you and a child play five card games over a course of time. Children like tallying how many wins and losses each player has and determining a winner at the end of the "series."

TIPS FOR PLAYING WITH ELEMENTARY-AGE CHILDREN

- Create interesting but fun and good-spirited competitions with children. When they're bored, they often become interested in play when you say, "I bet I can jump rope more times than you." Emphasize these competitions as fun and laid back so that children can challenge themselves without feeling frustrated.

- 10- and 11-year-olds often enjoy making model airplanes, rockets, and cars. Other older children like to tackle difficult art projects, such as candle making, tissue paper flowers, basket weaving, and sand art. These projects are good for children and help them develop a variety of skills including reading, following directions, spatial understanding, problem solving, creativity, and "stick-to-itiveness."

- Do creative activities together. Sometimes just having a box of materials (with paper, paints, markers, crayons, glue, and scissors) can keep you and a child happy and busy for hours.

ASSETS FOR INFANTS: A CHECKLIST

Think about your infant child or about each of the infants under your care. Check each statement that you feel is true. Use the checklist as a guide to show you where the infant is being well supported and where you need to build more assets for the infant. *NOTE: This checklist is a quick and informal way to raise awareness and prompt discussion. It is not intended as an accurate scientific measurement, and should not be used as such.*

_____ 1. The infant receives high levels of love and support from family members.

_____ 2. I communicate with the infant in positive ways. I respond immediately and respect the infant's needs.

_____ 3. I receive support from three or more adults, and I ask for help when needed. The infant receives additional love and comfort from at least one adult other than parents.

_____ 4. The infant experiences caring neighbors.

_____ 5. The infant is in caring, encouraging environments outside the home.

_____ 6. I am actively involved in communicating the infant's needs to caretakers and others in situations outside the home.

_____ 7. The family places the infant at the center of family life. Other adults in the community value and appreciate infants.

_____ 8. The family involves the infant in family life.

_____ 9. I serve others in the community.

_____ 10. The infant has a safe environment at home, in out-of-home settings, and in the neighborhood. This includes childproofing these environments.

_____ 11. I am aware of the infant's preferences and adapt the environment and schedule to suit the infant's needs. If the infant is mobile, I have begun to set limits.

_____ 12. Childcare settings and other out-of-home environments have clear rules and consequences for older infants and consistently provide all infants with appropriate stimulation and enough rest.

_____ 13. Neighbors take responsibility for monitoring and supervising the infant's behavior as the infant begins to play and interact outside the home.

_____ 14. I model positive, responsible behavior, and other adults in the infant's life do the same.

_____ 15. The infant observes siblings and other children interacting in positive ways. The infant has opportunities to interact with children of various ages.

_____ 16. I am realistic in my expectations for the child's development at this age. I encourage development without pushing the infant beyond his or her own pace.

_____ 17. I expose the infant to music, art, or other creative aspects of the environment each day.

_____ 18. I expose the infant to limited but stimulating situations outside the home. The family keeps the infant's needs in mind when attending events.

_____ 19. The family regularly attends religious programs or services while keeping the infant's needs in mind.

_____ 20. I supervise the infant at all times and provide predictable, enjoyable routines at home.

_____ 21. Family members are motivated to do well at work, at school, and in the community and model this motivation for the infant.

_____ 22. The family models responsive and attentive attitudes at work, at school, in the community, and at home.

_____ 23. I encourage the infant to explore, and I provide stimulating toys that match the infant's emerging skills. I am sensitive to the infant's disposition, preferences, and level of development.

_____ 24. I enjoy learning, and I model this through my own learning activities.

_____ 25. I read to the infant in enjoyable ways every day.

_____ 26. I convey my beliefs about helping others by modeling helping behaviors.

_____ 27. I place a high value on promoting social equality, religious tolerance, and reducing hunger and poverty while modeling these beliefs.

_____ 28. I act on my convictions, stand up for my beliefs, and communicate and model this in the family.

_____ 29. I tell the truth and convey my belief in honesty through my actions.

_____ 30. I accept and take personal responsibility.

_____ 31. I love the infant, setting the foundation for the infant to develop healthy attitudes and beliefs about relationships. I model, monitor, and teach the importance of good health habits, and I provide good nutritional choices and adequate rest and playtime.

_____ 32. I make all safety and care decisions for the infant and model safe behavior. I allow the infant to make simple choices as the infant becomes more independently mobile.

_____ 33. I model positive and constructive interactions with other people. I accept and am responsive to the infant's expression of feelings, seeing those expressions as cues to the infant's needs.

_____ 34. I know and am comfortable with people of different cultural, racial, and/or ethnic backgrounds, and I model this to the infant.

_____ 35. I model resistance skills through my own behaviors.

_____ 36. I behave in acceptable, nonviolent ways and assist the infant in developing these skills by helping the infant solve problems when faced with challenging or frustrating circumstances.

_____ 37. I feel I have control over things that happen in my own life, and I model coping skills, demonstrating healthy ways to deal with frustrations and challenges. I respond to the infant so the infant begins to learn that she or he has influence over immediate surroundings.

_____ 38. I create an environment where the infant can develop positive self-esteem, giving the infant appropriate, positive feedback and reinforcement about skills and competencies.

_____ 39. My life has purpose and I demonstrate this belief through my behaviors. The infant is curious about the world around him or her.

_____ 40. I am hopeful and positive about my personal future, and I work to provide a positive future for the infant.

ASSETS FOR TODDLERS: A CHECKLIST

Think about your toddler child or about each of the toddlers under your care. Check each statement that you feel is true. Use the checklist as a guide to show you where the toddler is being well supported and where you need to build more assets for the child. *NOTE: This checklist is a quick and informal way to raise awareness and prompt discussion. It is not intended as an accurate scientific measurement, and should not be used as such.*

_____ 1. The toddler receives high levels of love and support from family members.

_____ 2. I communicate with the toddler in positive ways. I respond to the toddler's needs in a reasonable amount of time and respect those needs.

_____ 3. I receive support from three or more adults, and I ask for help when needed. The toddler receives additional love and comfort from at least one adult other than parents.

_____ 4. The toddler experiences caring neighbors.

_____ 5. The toddler is in caring, encouraging environments outside the home.

_____ 6. I am actively involved in helping the toddler succeed in situations outside the home. I communicate the toddler's needs to caretakers outside the home.

_____ 7. The family places the toddler at the center of family life and recognizes the need to set limits for the toddler. Other adults in the community value and appreciate toddlers.

_____ 8. The family involves the toddler in family life.

_____ 9. I serve others in the community.

_____ 10. The toddler has a safe environment at home, in out-of-home settings, and in the neighborhood. This includes childproofing these environments.

_____ 11. I am aware of the toddler's preferences and adapt the environment to suit the toddler's needs. I set age-appropriate limits for the toddler.

_____ 12. Childcare settings and other out-of-home environments have clear rules and consequences to protect the toddler while consistently providing appropriate stimulation and enough rest.

_____ 13. Neighbors take responsibility for monitoring and supervising the toddler's behavior as the toddler begins to play and interact outside the home.

_____ 14. I model positive, responsible behavior, and other adults in the toddler's life do the same.

_____ 15. The toddler observes siblings and other children interacting in positive ways. The toddler has opportunities to interact with children of various ages.

_____ 16. I am realistic in my expectations for the child's development at this age. I encourage development without pushing the toddler beyond his or her own pace.

_____ 17. I expose the toddler to music, art, or other creative age-appropriate activities each day.

_____ 18. I expose the toddler to limited but stimulating situations outside the home. The family keeps the toddler's needs in mind when attending events.

_____ 19. The family regularly attends religious programs or services while keeping the toddler's needs in mind.

_____ 20. I supervise the toddler at all times and provide predictable, enjoyable routines at home.

_____ 21. Family members are motivated to do well at work, at school, and in the community and model this motivation for the toddler.

_____ 22. The family models responsive and attentive attitudes at work, at school, in the community, and at home.

_____ 23. I encourage the toddler to explore, and I provide stimulating toys that match the toddler's emerging skills. I am sensitive to the toddler's disposition, preferences, and level of development.

_____ 24. I enjoy learning, and I demonstrate this through my own learning activities.

_____ 25. I read to the toddler in enjoyable ways every day.

_____ 26. I convey my beliefs about helping others by modeling helping behaviors.

_____ 27. I place a high value on promoting social equality, religious tolerance, and reducing hunger and poverty while modeling these beliefs.

_____ 28. I act on my convictions, stand up for my beliefs, and communicate and model this in the family.

_____ 29. I tell the truth and convey my belief in honesty through my actions.

_____ 30. I accept and take personal responsibility.

_____ 31. I love the toddler, setting the foundation for the toddler to develop healthy attitudes and beliefs about relationships. I model, monitor, and teach the importance of good health habits, and provide good nutritional choices and adequate rest and playtime.

_____ 32. I make all safety and care decisions for the toddler and model safe behavior. I allow the toddler to make simple choices as the toddler becomes more independently mobile.

_____ 33. I model positive and constructive interactions with other people. I accept and am responsive to the how the toddler uses actions and words to express feelings, seeing those expressions as cues of the toddler's needs.

_____ 34. I know and am comfortable with people of different cultural, racial, and/or ethnic backgrounds, and model this to the toddler.

_____ 35. I model resistance skills through my own behavior. I am not overwhelmed by the toddler's needs, and I demonstrate appropriate resistance skills.

_____ 36. I behave in acceptable, nonviolent ways and assist the toddler in developing these skills by helping the toddler solve problems when faced with challenging or frustrating circumstances.

_____ 37. I feel I have control over things that happen in my own life, and I model coping skills, demonstrating healthy ways to deal with frustrations and challenges. I respond to the toddler so the toddler begins to learn that she or he has influence over immediate surroundings.

_____ 38. I create an environment where the toddler can develop positive self-esteem, giving the toddler appropriate, positive feedback and reinforcement about skills and competencies.

_____ 39. My life has purpose and I demonstrate this belief through my behaviors. The toddler is curious about the world around him or her.

_____ 40. I am hopeful and positive about my personal future, and I work to provide a positive future for the toddler.

ASSETS FOR PRESCHOOLERS: A CHECKLIST

Think about your preschool child or about each of the preschoolers under your care. Check each statement that you feel is true. Use the checklist as a guide to show you where the preschooler is being well supported and where you need to build more assets for the child. *NOTE: This checklist is a quick and informal way to raise awareness and prompt discussion. It is not intended as an accurate scientific measurement, and should not be used as such.*

_____ 1. The preschooler receives high levels of love and support from family members.

_____ 2. My preschooler and I communicate positively. My child seeks me out for help with difficult tasks or situations.

_____ 3. The preschooler receives support from at least one adult other than parents. I have support from people outside the home.

_____ 4. The preschooler experiences caring neighbors.

_____ 5. The preschooler is in caring, encouraging environments outside the home.

_____ 6. I am actively involved in helping the preschooler succeed in situations outside the home. I communicate the preschooler's needs to caretakers outside the home.

_____ 7. I value and appreciate preschoolers, and other adults in the community do, too.

_____ 8. I create ways the preschooler can help out, and I gradually include the child in age-appropriate tasks.

_____ 9. The family serves others in the community together.

_____ 10. The preschooler has a safe environment at home, in out-of-home settings, and in the neighborhood. This includes childproofing these environments.

_____ 11. The family has clear rules and consequences. The family monitors the child and consistently demonstrates appropriate behavior through modeling and limit setting.

_____ 12. Childcare settings and other out-of-home environments have clear rules and consequences to protect preschoolers while consistently providing appropriate stimulation and enough rest.

_____ 13. Neighbors take responsibility for monitoring and supervising the preschooler's behavior as the child begins to play and interact outside the home.

_____ 14. I model positive, responsible behavior, and other adults in the preschooler's life do the same.

_____ 15. I encourage the preschooler to play and interact with other children in safe, well-supervised settings.

_____ 16. I have realistic expectations for the child's development at this age. I encourage the preschooler to achieve and develop his or her unique talents, and caregivers and other adults do the same.

_____ 17. The preschooler participates in music, art, dramatic play, or other creative activities each day.

_____ 18. The preschooler interacts in stimulating ways with children outside the family. The family keeps the preschooler's needs in mind when attending events.

_____ 19. The family regularly attends religious programs or services while keeping the preschooler's needs in mind.

_____ 20. The preschooler is supervised by an adult at all times. The child spends most evenings and weekends at home with parents in predictable, enjoyable routines.

_____ 21. I convey and reinforce expectations to do well at work, at school, in the community, and within the family. Other adults do the same.

_____ 22. Family members model responsive and attentive attitudes at work, at school, in the community, and at home.

_____ 23. I encourage the preschooler to explore, and I provide stimulating toys that match the child's emerging skills. I am sensitive to the preschooler's disposition, preferences, and level of development.

_____ 24. I enjoy learning and engage the preschooler in learning activities. Other adults do the same.

_____ 25. An adult reads to the preschooler for at least 30 minutes over the course of a day, encouraging the child to participate.

_____ 26. I encourage the preschooler to express sympathy for someone who is distressed and to begin to develop a variety of helping behaviors.

_____ 27. I place a high value on promoting social equality, religious tolerance, and reducing hunger and poverty while modeling these beliefs.

_____ 28. I act on my convictions, stand up for my beliefs, and communicate and model this in the family.

_____ 29. The preschooler is learning the difference between telling the truth and lying.

_____ 30. The preschooler is learning that actions affect on other people.

_____ 31. I model, monitor, and teach the importance of good health habits. Other adults do the same. The preschooler is beginning to learn healthy sexual attitudes and beliefs as well as respect for others.

_____ 32. The preschooler is beginning to make simple choices, solve simple problems, and develop simple plans at an age-appropriate level.

_____ 33. The preschooler plays and interacts with other children and adults. The child freely expresses feelings and is learning to put these feelings into words. I model and teach empathy, and other adults do the same.

_____ 34. The preschooler is exposed in positive ways to information about and to people of different cultural, racial, and/or ethnic backgrounds.

_____ 35. The preschooler is taught to resist participating in inappropriate or dangerous behavior.

_____ 36. I model positive ways to resolve conflicts, and other adults do the same. The preschooler is taught and is beginning to practice nonviolent, acceptable ways to deal with challenging and frustrating situations.

_____ 37. I feel I have control over things that happen in my own life, and I model coping skills, demonstrating healthy ways to deal with frustrations and challenges. I respond to the preschooler so the child begins to learn that she or he has influence over immediate surroundings.

_____ 38. I create an environment where the preschooler can develop positive self-esteem, giving the child appropriate positive feedback and reinforcement about skills and competencies.

_____ 39. My life has purpose and I demonstrate this belief through my behaviors. The preschooler is curious and explores the world around him or her.

_____ 40. I am hopeful and positive about my personal future, and I work to provide a positive future for the preschooler.

ASSETS FOR ELEMENTARY-AGE CHILDREN: A CHECKLIST

Think about your elementary-age child or about each of the elementary-age children under your care. Check each statement that you feel is true. Use the checklist as a guide to show you where the child is being well supported and where you need to build more assets for the child. *NOTE: This checklist is a quick and informal way to raise awareness and prompt discussion. It is not intended as an accurate scientific measurement, and should not be used as such.*

_____ 1. The child receives high levels of love and support from family members.

_____ 2. My child and I communicate positively. My child is willing to seek me out for advice and counsel.

_____ 3. The child receives support from adults other than parents.

_____ 4. The child experiences caring neighbors.

_____ 5. School and other activities provide caring, encouraging environments for the child.

_____ 6. I am actively involved in helping my child succeed in school and in other situations outside the home.

_____ 7. The child feels that the family and community value and appreciate children.

_____ 8. The child is included in age-appropriate family tasks and decisions and is given useful roles at home and in the community.

_____ 9. The child serves others and the community with the family or in other settings.

_____ 10. The child is safe at home, at school, and in the neighborhood.

_____ 11. The family has clear rules and consequences and monitors the child's activities and whereabouts.

_____ 12. School and other out-of-home environments provide clear rules and consequences.

_____ 13. Neighbors take responsibility for monitoring the child's behavior.

_____ 14. I model positive, responsible behavior, and other adults in the child's life do the same.

_____ 15. The child interacts with other children who model responsible behavior and has opportunities to play and interact in safe, well-supervised settings.

_____ 16. I have realistic expectations for the child's development at this age. I encourage the child to achieve and develop unique talents, and caregivers and other adults do the same.

_____ 17. The child participates in music, art, drama, or other creative activity for at least three hours a week at home and elsewhere.

_____ 18. The child spends one hour or more each week in extracurricular school activities or structured community programs.

_____ 19. The family attends religious programs or services for at least one hour per week.

_____ 20. The child spends most evenings and weekends at home with parents in predictable, enjoyable routines.

_____ 21. The child is motivated to do well in school and other activities.

_____ 22. The child is responsive, attentive, and actively engaged in learning.

_____ 23. I encourage the child to explore and engage in stimulating activities, and teachers do the same. The child does homework when it's assigned.

_____ 24. The child enjoys learning and cares about the school.

_____ 25. The child and an adult read together for at least 30 minutes a day. The child also enjoys reading or looking at books or magazines independently.

_____ 26. The child is encouraged to help other people.

_____ 27. The child is beginning to show interest in making the community a better place.

_____ 28. The child is beginning to act on convictions and stand up for personal beliefs.

_____ 29. The child is beginning to value honesty and act accordingly.

_____ 30. The child is beginning to accept and take personal responsibility for age-appropriate tasks.

_____ 31. The child is beginning to value good health habits and learn healthy sexual attitudes and beliefs as well as respect for others.

_____ 32. The child is beginning to learn how to plan ahead and make choices at an appropriate developmental level.

_____ 33. The child interacts with adults and children and can make friends. The child expresses and articulates feelings in appropriate ways and empathizes with others.

_____ 34. The child knows about and is comfortable with people of different cultural, racial, and/or ethnic backgrounds.

_____ 35. The child starts to develop the ability to resist negative peer pressure and dangerous situations.

_____ 36. The child tries to resolve conflicts nonviolently.

_____ 37. The child begins to feel a sense of control over things that happen to him or her. The child is beginning to manage frustrations and challenges in ways that have positive results for the child and others.

_____ 38. The child reports having high self-esteem.

_____ 39. The child reports that "my life has a purpose" and actively engages her or his skills.

_____ 40. The child is hopeful and positive about his or her personal future.

25 WAYS TO BUILD ASSETS IN INFANTS

1. Respond to infants' needs immediately.
2. Hold infants and interact with them during feedings.
3. Show your delight in each infant's growth and development.
4. Always supervise and monitor infants to keep them safe.
5. Find out what infants are communicating when they cry.
6. Prop infants up so they can see more.
7. Distract infants from inappropriate behavior and draw attention to appropriate behavior.
8. Infants have reasons for the things they do. They pull on an earring because it looks interesting. They squish food all over their tray because it feels good in their fingers. They shriek to hear the sound of their voice. They bat at someone's face because they can't fully control their movements. Sometimes adults think that actions like these are "misbehavior." They're not. Infants don't hurt people, make a mess, or create an annoying racket on purpose. They do these things because they come naturally to babies at this stage of life.
9. Encourage new milestones, such as crawling and standing, without pushing infants when they aren't yet ready.
10. Make sure infants spend most of their time with their parents or one or two consistent caregivers.
11. Be flexible with an infant's schedule and gradually introduce predictable routines.
12. Monitor activity carefully at this age. It's easy for an infant to become understimulated or over-stimulated. When babies turn away, shut their eyes, or become fussy, they're often overstimulated. Babies also tend to become fussy when they don't have enough activity. When an infant seems upset, be aware of what's going on in the environment.
13. Expose babies to new environments, such as parks and stores.
14. Sing and read to babies daily.
15. Provide new, interesting things for infants to look at, such as toys in different colors, shapes, and sizes.
16. Create a caring atmosphere at home, in childcare centers and nurseries, and in other places where infants spend time.
17. Talk to all family members about your values. Model and teach values as infants grow. For example, feed infants nutritious foods, and eat healthy foods yourself. Talk with the family about how these choices build Asset 31: Family Values Healthy Lifestyle.
18. Treat all infants equally. Be excited about all the infants you see.
19. Encourage older infants to experiment with sounds and with touching new things.
20. Affirm infants as they learn new skills.
21. As infants start to eat solids, expose them to new foods a little at a time.
22. Love, respect, and accept infants unconditionally.
23. Get to know and enjoy each infant's unique personality.
24. Create positive interactions. Play together in ways that make infants laugh and enjoy the time together. Play with fingers and toes. Gently poke an infant's tummy or chubby knees. Show an older infant how to play "Pat-a-Cake."
25. Have fun with infants. Rock them. Play peek-a-boo. Crawl after them on the floor.

25 WAYS TO BUILD ASSETS IN TODDLERS

1. Cheer on toddlers as they master new skills and milestones.
2. Be available to comfort and guide toddlers when they become frustrated, but also allow them to master new and challenging age-appropriate skills.
3. Show toddlers that you're excited by their discoveries about themselves, other people, and the world.
4. Say "yes" to toddlers more than you say "no." Choose carefully those times when you must say "no."
5. Encourage the concept of helping others by having toddlers do simple tasks, such as tearing lettuce or putting napkins on plates.
6. Ensure safety by childproofing all areas where toddlers play.
7. Show toddlers positive alternatives to inappropriate behaviors. Encourage them to use their expanding language skills.
8. Expose toddlers to other toddlers, but don't expect them to know how to play together. Supervise and help them learn to do this a little at a time.
9. Give simple, understandable boundaries, such as "Don't bite" or "Please be quiet."
10. Enforce boundaries and limits consistently. For example, always place toddlers in a car seat. Some toddlers don't like being restrained in the car, but be firm about safety issues like this one. Never let a toddler sit on your lap while riding in a car, even if you're going only a short distance.
11. As much as possible, have regular times for toddlers to sleep, eat, play, and relax.
12. Balance stimulating, structured time with free playtime.
13. Find ways to have positive, meaningful family times at home with toddlers.
14. Make a game out of learning the names of objects.
15. Help toddlers group objects according to similarities, such as shape, size, or color.
16. Whenever you're with a toddler, talk about what you see, and ask the toddler to talk about what he or she sees, too.
17. When toddlers act inappropriately, *show* them a better way to act.
18. Help toddlers find simple ways to show that they care for others—such as giving a sibling a hug or petting an animal gently.
19. If a toddler has a temper tantrum, take the child to a quiet place to settle down. Hold the child firmly but not harshly. Keep your voice steady and calm.
20. Allow toddlers to express their feelings, but give them guidelines on appropriate and inappropriate ways to act on them. ("You're mad at the puppy because she won't play with you. She doesn't like to have her tail pulled—that hurts. Try patting her back gently, instead.")
21. Whenever possible, give toddlers at least two equally appealing choices.
22. Ask toddlers what their favorite songs are. Sing the songs together.
23. Do not blame or shame toddlers when correcting their inappropriate behavior. Focus on the action, not the child. ("That wasn't a nice thing to do. It's not okay to throw blocks at people.")
24. Focus on what toddlers do right instead of what they do wrong. Applaud their new skills.
25. Interact with toddlers in loving, respectful, and caring ways.

25 WAYS TO BUILD ASSETS IN PRESCHOOLERS

1. Play with preschoolers, letting them choose the type of play.
2. Find other caring adults to participate regularly in preschoolers' lives.
3. Encourage preschoolers' thinking abilities by exposing them to new situations, such as visiting a beach, a construction site, an apple orchard, or a children's museum.
4. Do simple acts of community service together, such as collecting cans of food for a food bank.
5. Teach preschoolers basic safety rules, such as avoiding poisons and looking both ways before crossing the street while holding an adult's hand.
6. Give preschoolers simple chores, such as sorting laundry by color or matching socks.
7. Encourage preschoolers to play with another child on a regular basis. This helps children learn social skills.
8. Stay calm when preschoolers act in highly emotional ways.
9. Demonstrate appropriate behaviors rather than just telling preschoolers what to do and what not to do. ("We wait our turn in line, like this.")
10. Follow preschoolers' lead in which activities interest them most. Support that interest by exposing children to other related activities. For example, if a child likes insects, go on walks where you identify them, search for books about them, and draw or paint them.
11. Introduce preschoolers to zoos, children's story hours, preschool programs, and other events that welcome young children.
12. Look for fun ways to play together as a family.
13. Give preschoolers opportunities to meet and spend time with a neighbor, a great-aunt or great-uncle, or another adult who's important to you.
14. Visit the library often. Have preschoolers choose books to check out.
15. Make up new songs, stories, and games to play with preschoolers.
16. Notice and comment on preschoolers' appropriate behavior.
17. Teach preschoolers how to care for a special toy, outfit, pet, or plant, but don't expect preschoolers to do this on their own. They'll need an adult's active participation.
18. When you notice others behaving in ways you admire or don't admire, explain your own family's values to preschoolers. For example: "I like how that girl is sharing by giving her toy to the boy next to her."
19. Emphasize the concept of sharing. Model sharing whenever possible.
20. Continue to cheer on preschoolers' new skills, such as cutting, drawing, and walking backward.
21. Have periodic family meetings where preschoolers have input and a voice in decision making.
22. Ask preschoolers how they feel about the events in their lives. Encourage them to identify more positive examples than negative ones. Ask: "What makes you feel happy? When do you get excited?" Encourage preschoolers to articulate their feelings by using words.
23. Break new tasks and skills into small, manageable steps so that preschoolers can master them without becoming too frustrated. For example, you can teach learning to put on and buckle a shoe in four steps: First, put the left shoe on the left foot. Second, slide the shoe strap into the buckle. Third, push the buckle pin through the hole on the strap. Fourth, slide the strap through the other side of the buckle.
24. Encourage preschoolers to take pride in their cultural heritage. Share pictures and stories about children's background. Start or keep traditions that highlight this heritage.
25. Dress up with preschoolers. Pretend to be astronauts, doctors, and veterinarians. Help their imagination soar.

25 WAYS TO BUILD ASSETS IN ELEMENTARY-AGE CHILDREN

1. Answer children's questions.
2. Encourage children as they learn new skills.
3. When children and adults disagree, encourage adults to be respectful about the child's point of view. Reassure children that disagreements won't stop you from caring about them.
4. Closely monitor children and their activities. While they don't need constant, *direct* supervision, it's still important that adults keep an eye on what children are doing.
5. Ask children's opinions about what they like and don't like in their daily routines. If it's possible, make changes to accommodate some of their wishes.
6. Ask children how they would like to help others. Figure out simple ways for them to carry through and do this.
7. Be firm about boundaries you've set, especially those that ensure children's safety.
8. Be consistent with the consequences for violating limits and boundaries.
9. Make sure that schools, activity leaders, and community organizations set and maintain consistent boundaries and consequences.
10. Set aside a family night at least once a month to do something fun together.
11. Allow children to have one or two out-of-home activities (such as participating in a team sport and playing a musical instrument) that are led by caring, nurturing adults.
12. Help children to begin to balance their time so they gradually learn how to keep from overbooking or underbooking their schedules.
13. Set daily homework guidelines and arrange a quiet workplace where children can study.
14. As children learn to read, ask them to read to you every day.
15. Visit new places with children to expose them to different cultures, people, and experiences.
16. Participate in service activities together as a family or group.
17. When children ask about sexuality or about alcohol and other drugs, answer the questions accurately and with simple language. Ask children if they would like more information, and respect their answer. Most children need to learn about these sophisticated subjects a little at a time, so keep the door open for more conversations.
18. When children receive gifts, have them write thank-you notes or show their appreciation in other ways, perhaps with a phone call or by making a simple gift in return.
19. Emphasize that children should use words to make their needs known. Remind children that hitting or other violent activities are not acceptable.
20. Restrain yourself from jumping in to help children do new or difficult things. Allow children opportunities to succeed and fail.
21. Encourage children to develop more skills in areas that interest them.
22. Ask children how they feel about their future. Encourage them to take concrete steps to make their future something positive to look forward to. For instance, if children worry about pollution, volunteer to help clean up a park or roadside together. If they worry about hunger, get involved gathering food or stocking it at a food shelf. Point out the progress you make while you're working.
23. Encourage children to seek out answers and solutions when they face obstacles or difficult times. Be available to help, and guide children to other supportive adults and resources as well.
24. Have children identify people of good character, famous or not, to be their role models.
25. On a regular basis, give children your undivided attention for a block of time. Ask them what they would like to do with you, and then do that together.

FIRST STEPS FOR INFANTS

Infants need people around them to guide their steps and to walk side by side with them as they journey through life. Look at the words below. They all describe different ways to bring out the best in infants by building assets. Circle ideas that you can begin doing right now—and start building assets.

Make mealtimes, bedtimes, and changing times fun.

Repeat the sounds infants make.

Pick infants up and dance to music. Choose country, jazz, or classical.

Sing to infants.

Look in infants' eyes when you talk to them.

Crawl with infants.

Hold infants to your shoulder so they have a better view.

Gently massage infants as you bathe them.

Always have an open lap.

Play peek-a-boo.

Take infants for a stroller ride.

Rock infants.

Look in a mirror together.

Splash in water together.

Play with infants' hands and feet.

Cheer infants on as they explore new objects.

Let infants grasp your fingers.

Read to infants.

Hold infants' hands to support them as they learn to walk.

Hold infants.

Give infants mobiles to look at.

With older infants, hide objects for them to find.

Meet infants' needs.

Celebrate the milestones infants master, like crawling and walking.

Be relaxed with infants.

Give infants toys that rattle, make noise, or play music.

Smile at infants.

FIRST STEPS FOR TODDLERS

Toddlers need people around them to guide their steps and to walk side by side with them as they journey through life. Look at the words below. They all describe different ways to bring out the best in toddlers by building assets. Circle ideas that you can begin doing right now—and start building assets.

Use your imagination together.
Take a drink from an empty cup.
Flap your arms and "fly."

Go on a "What's that?" hunt. Ask toddlers what they see.

Visit a playground.

Wink at toddlers.

Look in toddlers' eyes when you talk to them.

Play with dolls and cars and trucks.

Sing with toddlers.

Invite toddlers to color, and praise their marks and designs.

Look at photographs together.

Ask toddlers where their feet, hands, eyes, and ears are.

Smile at toddlers.

Go for a walk together.

Go hunting for ants.

Put on music to dance to.

Wash and dry your hands together.

Finger paint together.

Follow a toddler up the stairs.

Say "yes" a lot.

Remember toddlers' birthdays.

Read books together.
Let toddlers turn the pages.

Blow bubbles for toddlers to chase.

Build a block tower together.

Chase toddlers.

Play with clay or dough together.

Roll a ball to toddlers and encourage them to kick or roll it back.

Splash in water together.

Dress a doll or teddy bear together.

Make a game by using your quietest inside voices when you're indoors and your loudest outside voices when you're not.

Be relaxed around toddlers.

FIRST STEPS FOR PRESCHOOLERS

Preschoolers need people around them to guide their steps and to walk side by side with them as they journey through life. Look at the words below. They all describe different ways to bring out the best in preschoolers by building assets. Circle ideas that you can begin doing right now—and start building assets.

Visit a playground.

Ask preschoolers about their favorite color, animal, book, and food.

Sing with preschoolers. Let them pick the song.

Compare shoes.

Smile at preschoolers.

Read picture books with colorful illustrations and photographs.

Play hide-and-seek together.

Bake cookies together.

Ask preschoolers about themselves.

Splash in a wading pool.

Look in preschoolers' eyes when you talk to them.

Give high fives.

Have puppet shows.

Play a preschool-friendly board game like "Candyland" together.

Pick dandelion bouquets.

Dress up.

Go for a walk together.

Go to a museum, park, zoo, or other interesting place.

Color together.

Make funny noises together.

Blow bubbles together.

Eat ice cream for a treat.

Play doctor and put bandages all over each other.

Drink imaginary tea with preschoolers.

Give each other a new hairdo.

Meet preschoolers' stuffed animals, action figures, and dolls.

Remember preschoolers' birthdays.

Set your worries aside and focus only on the child.

Plant seeds together.

Play singing games, such as "London Bridge" or "Ring Around the Rosie."

FIRST STEPS FOR ELEMENTARY-AGE CHILDREN

Elementary-age children need people around them to guide their steps and to walk side by side with them as they journey through life. Look at the words below. They all describe different ways to bring out the best in children by building assets. Circle ideas that you can begin doing right now—and start building assets.

Smile at children.

Go out for breakfast—or lunch. Let children choose where they want to eat.

Hang up children's artwork at home or at work.

Remember children's birthdays.

Play together outside. Play catch with a large ball or a football.

Go to a museum, park, zoo, or other interesting place.

Visit the library together.

Meet children's friends.

Invite children to read aloud to you.

Look in children's eyes when you talk to them.

Do magic tricks.

Make pizza together.

Eat candy for a treat.

Listen to children's favorite music with them.

Go on a bike ride.

Jump rope together.

Take children to the beach or a swimming pool.

Meet children's pets.

Ask to see a child's collection. Contribute to it.

Play a card game.

Grow pumpkins together.

Ask children questions about their families.

Play a board game together. Let children choose the game.

Send children postcards or letters in the mail.

Find an interesting craft to do together.

Watch a TV show together.

Ask children about what they like to do best.

Just for fun, chew bubble gum together. Make the gum snap. Have a bubble-blowing contest.

Laugh at children's knock-knock jokes.

YOUR ASSET-BUILDING JOURNEY

Throughout your life, you've had activities, experiences, and relationships with people who built your assets. In the suitcase spaces below, list what and who these asset-building experiences involved, and where they took place. For example, your scout meeting place or piano teacher's living room may have been asset-building places. Performing in a play, reading a highly influential book, or getting an article published in your school newspaper may have been asset-building activities. A coach and a teacher may have been people who built your assets.

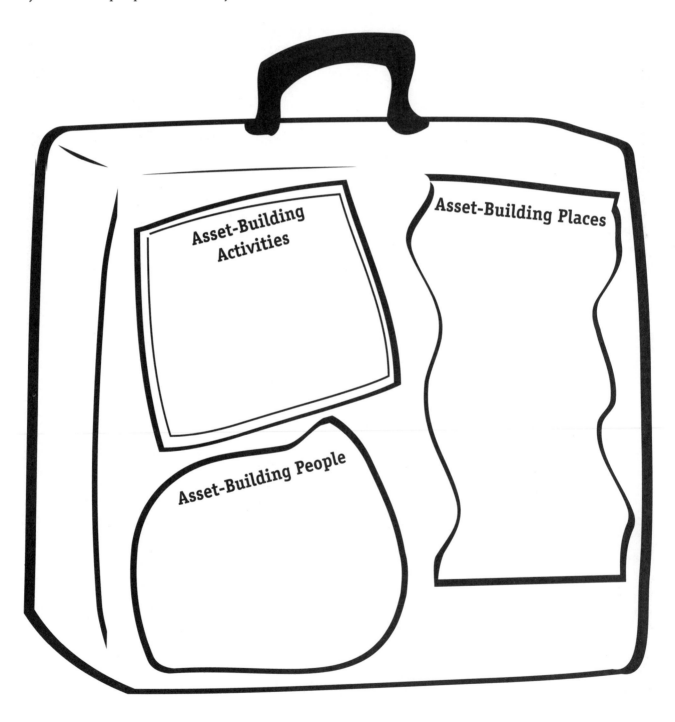

THE ABCs AND XYZs OF BUILDING YOUNG CHILDREN'S ASSETS

Amaze children with extraordinary and everyday experiences.

Boost children's enthusiasm for learning.

Comment on children's new skills and appropriate behavior.

Delight in children's discoveries.

Ease children into new situations and challenges.

Fascinate children with memorable stories.

Giggle and laugh together.

Hang out with children.

Inspire children's creativity.

Join children in their adventures.

Keep children safe.

Love children—no matter what.

Magnify children's magnificence (their accomplishments and kind acts) with encouragement and praise.

Notice children.

Open up possibilities for children.

Pamper children when they're sick, sad, or crabby.

Quote children's remarkable sayings.

Recognize the incredible—and the commonplace—things children do.

Surround children with caring, inspiring people.

Thank children when they act in kind or generous ways.

Understand children's points of view by listening to what they say.

Value who children are and what they want to do.

Wonder at children's ideas and insights.

e**X**plore new places and activities with children.

Yodel with children. Sing, chant, and make up songs together.

Zero in on what makes each child unique—and terrific!

EASY IDEAS FOR BUILDING ASSETS IN ALL YOUNG CHILDREN: A WORKSHEET

It's easier to build assets in children we're comfortable with than it is to reach out to children we don't know well. But every child needs assets, and every child needs lots of adults to help build them in large—and small—way. Focus on simple, small ways to build assets. Think of a few easy ways you can begin to build assets in all the children you see or meet. Use this handout as a starting point.

Infants
Birth to 12 Months

Infants around you:	Easy ideas to consider: Send a card or gift at birth. Visit an infant. Hold an infant. Coo at an infant.	Your one easy idea:

Toddlers
Ages 13 to 35 Months

Toddlers around you:	Easy ideas to consider: Ask toddlers what they see around them. Play a clapping game with a toddler. Color with a toddler. Smile at a toddler.	Your one easy idea:

Preschoolers
Ages 3 to 5 Years

Preschoolers around you:	Easy ideas to consider: Learn preschoolers' names. Say hi to preschoolers. Chase preschoolers. Ask about a preschooler's favorite toy.	Your one easy idea:

Elementary-Age Children
Ages 6 to 11 Years

Elementary-age children around you:	Easy ideas to consider: Ask about children's interests. Clip comic strips for children. Attend children's activities. Tell a child a knock-knock joke.	Your one easy idea:

FACTS ABOUT YOUNG CHILDREN AND ASSETS

A number of research studies back up the concepts of the developmental assets framework for children. Here are some research highlights:

SUPPORT

Parents who answered infants' cries immediately and consistently during the first few months of life had infants who cried less frequently and for shorter periods of time than parents who did not respond quickly. Silvia M. Bell and Mary D.S. Ainsworth, "Infant Crying and Maternal Responsiveness," *Child Development* 43, no. 4 (1972), pages 1171–1190.

EMPOWERMENT

Children develop independence, self-reliance, and positive self-esteem when parents involve them in developmentally appropriate household tasks and in age-appropriate family decisions. Charlotte R. Wallinga and Anne L. Sweaney, "A Sense of Real Accomplishment: Young Children as Productive Family Members," *Young Children* 41, no. 1 (1985), pages 3–8.

BOUNDARIES AND EXPECTATIONS

Toddlers who are given clear limits, whose parents try to promote sympathy and compassion for others, and who are taught how to behave by being given instructions and explanations are more likely to comply with parents' requests than children who have been threatened or physically punished. These findings were reported by researchers at the National Institute of Mental Health. Leon Kuczynski and Grazyna Kochanska, "Development of Children's Non-Compliance Strategies from Toddlerhood to Age 5," *Developmental Psychology* 26 (1990), pages 398–408.

CONSTRUCTIVE USE OF TIME

Not only do the quality of play materials and daily experiences with music, art, and drama add pleasure to a child's life, but they also are predictors of achievement test scores in fourth and fifth grades. Robert H. Bradley, Bettye M. Caldwell, and Stephen L. Rock, "Home Environment and School Performance: A Ten-Year Follow-Up Examination of Three Models of Environmental Action," *Child Development* 59 (1988), pages 852–867.

COMMITMENT TO LEARNING

Children whose parents play with them and provide them with high-quality, age-appropriate toys during infancy, toddlerhood, and preschool tend to do well in school. Robert H. Bradley, Bettye M. Caldwell, and Stephen L. Rock, "Home Environment and School Performance: A Ten-Year Follow-Up Examination of Three Models of Environmental Action," *Child Development* 59 (1988), pages 852–867.

POSITIVE VALUES

Toddlers are capable of sympathy, which is an early step toward altruism (unselfish concern for the welfare of others). Toddlers will offer a toy to a companion, help with household chores, or demonstrate compassion by trying to cheer up a distressed playmate. Harriet L. Rheingold, "Little Children's Participation in the Work of Adults, and Nascent Prosocial Behavior," *Child Development* 53 (1982), pages 114–125.

FACTS ABOUT YOUNG CHILDREN AND ASSETS

SOCIAL COMPETENCIES

Families who express and describe their feelings raised children who were more likely to identify their own feelings and those of others, a crucial social skill. Judy Dunn, Jane Brown, and Lynn Beardsall, "Family Talk about Feeling States and Children's Later Understanding of Children's Emotions," *Developmental Psychology* 27 (1991), pages 448–455.

POSITIVE IDENTITY

A child's self-esteem is affected by how competent the child feels in the domains (areas) he or she considers particularly important, says researcher Susan Harter. For example, if playing softball is important to a young girl, and she feels that she's good at softball, her self-esteem will likely be affected positively. Susan Harter, "Self and Identity Development," in *At the Threshold: The Developing Adolescent*, edited by Shirley S. Feldman and Glen R. Elliott (Cambridge, MA: Harvard University Press, 1990), pages 353–387.

ASSET-BUILDING TIPS FOR YOUNG CHILDREN WITH SPECIAL NEEDS

The asset framework emphasizes the development of the whole child. The 40 developmental assets can help bring out the best in all children, including those with special needs. Here are some ideas for supporting children with learning differences or other special needs:

- Develop expectations that aren't too high or too low. Expect children to grow and develop, but adjust your expectations to fit their individual needs and unique circumstances.

- Encourage children to articulate their needs and feelings. For example, children may become frustrated easily and may need additional help with certain tasks.

- Because of their different behavior or learning style, children may receive a lot of negative feedback. This may lead children to focus on the ways they don't measure up instead of on the areas where they're succeeding. Give children lots of positive feedback about what they're doing well.

- Some children are highly emotional and struggle with how to deal with their emotions. Help children find appropriate ways to express feelings and cope with frustrations.

- Be aware that children with special needs may have low self-esteem. They may encounter situations where they are told that they're "not trying hard enough" or that they're "lazy" or "stupid." Find ways to help children feel good about who they are. Speak up and advocate for children if other adults don't adjust their expectations to fit the children's unique needs.

- Pay attention to children's actions. Children with learning disabilities may be slower to learn the social and language skills that help them articulate their needs. When they act in inappropriate ways, they may really be saying that they're frustrated, uncomfortable, sad, or angry. Help children identify what they're feeling.

- Help children see that they are much more than their academic achievement. Relating to other people, developing an interesting hobby, and being motivated to try new things are equally important.

- Set clear boundaries about what's acceptable for other people to say and not to say to children with special needs. *All* children need people who advocate and stand up for them and who model these skills so that they can learn how to treat others and advocate on their own behalf.

- Some children may withdraw or prefer to be with younger children. Encourage children not to withdraw from peers because of felt or imagined differences. Help them find ways to get along with other children. Give them opportunities to be with children who will accept them for who they are and to be involved in activities where they can shine.

- Support children by helping them to understand their own needs and to make their needs known. This gives children a sense of power to impact their own experiences.

- Be persistent and positive. "Most children with learning differences get better as they get older," write Gary Fisher, Ph.D., and Rhoda Cummings, Ed.D., in their book *When Your Child Has LD* (Minneapolis: Free Spirit Publishing, 1995, page 95). These authors say that identifying strategies to compensate for learning differences will help children be successful in the future.

- Children with special needs may require more structure and guidance than other children, particularly when it comes to homework. Set up a homework time and space. Teach children how to prioritize their activities.

- Build on children's strengths. Find out what they enjoy doing and what they excel at. If they're great at playing basketball, encourage them to develop those skills. Cheer on their achievements. All children have strengths.

ASSET-BUILDING TIPS FOR YOUNG GIFTED CHILDREN

The asset framework emphasizes the development of the whole child. The 40 developmental assets can help bring out the best in all children, including those with special abilities and talents. Here are some ideas for supporting gifted children:

- Encourage gifted children to keep asking questions. When you don't know the answers, do the research together.

- Because of their advanced academic abilities, gifted children may tend to spend their time with adults and older children. Create meaningful opportunities for gifted children to play with younger children and with children their own age.

- Affirm children's sense of equality and justice (Asset 27). For example, if a child wants to collect blankets for a homeless shelter, encourage the child to do so, and pitch in. Many gifted children have a strong sense of fairness and justice from a young age.

- Boundaries that are especially helpful to gifted children are those that do the following: balance children's tendency to be perfectionists (these children often set standards for themselves that are extremely high and difficult to meet), slow children down (they often have high energy and are used to learning quickly), and help them learn to be flexible (they tend to want to do one thing and nothing else). While a gifted child's long attention span is usually a plus, a child who becomes deeply absorbed in one activity may have difficulty making transitions to others.

- Emphasize and teach interpersonal skills (Asset 33). Gifted children sometimes struggle to connect with their peers. Sometimes they talk too much or at a level other children don't understand.

- Provide a lot of support. Although gifted children may seem self-confident and self-assured, they may try to appear in control by talking logically and with apparent insight when they're feeling scared or insecure.

- Concentrate on building Asset 40: Positive View of Personal Future. Due to their highly developed thinking skills, gifted children may take an overly critical attitude toward others or themselves. They can also feel acute worry or fear (about war, fire, pollution, violence, or child poverty) because they become aware of these issues at an early age but haven't developed the emotional skills for coping with the information.

- Encourage gifted children to follow their passions. When they become excited about a subject, they can spend hours learning about it. Share their enthusiasm.

- Keep finding new ways to stimulate gifted children. They may easily become bored. Visit historical sites, llama farms, raspberry fields, and interesting community events when children tire of zoos and libraries.

- Challenge gifted children academically. If they become bored with learning, create projects and assignments that stimulate their thinking. Teach them to challenge themselves. When they say they're bored, ask, "What can you do that wouldn't be boring?"

- Gifted children may have particular talents or capabilities in one or two areas or in a number of them. Encourage children to apply themselves to all subjects in school and to be willing to participate in a variety of activities, including those that don't come easily.

ASSET-BUILDING TIPS FOR YOUNG GIFTED CHILDREN

- Gifted children may be highly sensitive to sounds, smells, tastes, and other sensations. Respect these sensitivities. For example, help children cut the tags out of their shirts if these tags bother them, and point out that some children prefer loud events (such as sports and concerts) while others prefer quieter ones (such as going to the library).

- Support children and encourage them to engage in healthy challenges. Many gifted children hold back because they don't want to look foolish, be wrong, or show that they don't understand something.

- Encourage gifted children to be children. They need time to play, to be silly, and to relax.

- Be sensitive to the fact that gifted children may be one age intellectually, another age physically, another socially, and yet another emotionally. While this can apply to all children to a degree, it can be especially true for gifted kids. Don't emphasize only talents or intellectual abilities. Help children develop into well-rounded people by talking with them about feelings and helping them develop needed skills. By the same token, don't push skills a young child isn't ready to master.

- Build positive values in gifted children. Nurture their sense of caring and service. Encourage them to live a healthy lifestyle.

- Enjoy gifted children's discoveries and insights.

THE ASSET BUILDERS AROUND YOU

Every person has asset builders in their lives, and asset builders need other people to support and care for them. In the circles below, write the names of individuals who bring out the best in you—right now. If you can't think of many people, think about how you can reach out to other people and expand your support base. Thank the people who do support you, and tell them how much you appreciate having them in your life.

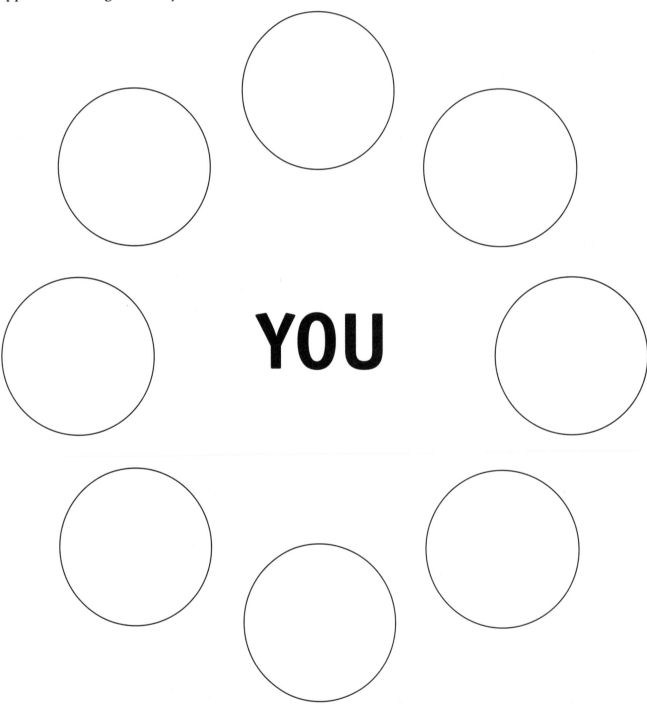

KEEPING CHILDREN SAFE

Use this checklist to ensure that children are safe from accidents and harm.

_____ Store medicines, household cleaners, poisons, and plastic bags out of reach in locked child-proof cabinets and containers.

_____ Keep all plastic bags and thin plastics (such as ones used by dry cleaners) away from young children.

_____ Place matches, lighters, and anything breakable out of children's reach.

_____ Never leave water in a sink or tub. Install safety latches on toilets so infants and young toddlers can't open them.

_____ Seal all unused electrical outlets with childproof covers. Move electrical cords out of reach of children.

_____ Use safety covers on stove and oven knobs. Keep handles of pots on the stove turned inward, away from small hands.

_____ Post a list of emergency numbers (including the local poison control center and the closest hospital) near every phone in the home.

_____ Install safety gates near all stairways.

_____ Keep infants safe by staying with them at all times when you have them on changing tables, tabletops, couches, or other high places. Infants can easily roll off elevated areas.

_____ Keep small objects away from children under the age of 3, since young children like to put small items into their mouths.

_____ When bathing an infant, place a washcloth or small towel at the bottom of the tub to keep the baby from slipping. Never leave a baby alone in a bath or near any pool of water, including wading pools and fish ponds.

_____ Place crib mattresses at the lowest settings. Keep the crib free of objects and away from items that young children could grab, such as drapes, mini-blind cords, hanging toys, and electrical cords.

_____ Never leave young children alone with a pet (even a gentle pet) or a young sibling.

_____ Leave young children in the care of a sitter who is at least 14 years old and who is trained in infant CPR and other safety guidelines.

_____ Never place a necklace or string holding a pacifier around a baby's neck.

_____ Remove all guns from the environments where children live, play, and spend time.

_____ Use approved, properly installed car seats. The safest place for a car seat is in the back seat. Car seats should be rear facing for children up to 20 pounds and front facing for children 20 pounds and over.

_____ Always stay with children in a car. Never leave them unattended.

_____ Place car seats and infant seats on the ground or floor when you take them out of the car. Otherwise they could easily topple over.

_____ Make sure environments away from home follow the safety standards listed above for the home.

_____ When playing with children on outdoor play equipment, make sure that the surface underneath the equipment is safe. The best surfaces are grass, sand, or wood chips.

KEEPING CHILDREN SAFE

_____ Teach children safe ways to cross streets. Insist that young children hold an adult's hand while crossing the street.

_____ Make sure that play areas for infants, toddlers, preschoolers, and younger elementary-age children are fenced.

_____ Always supervise young children's play.

_____ Insist that children use safety equipment such as life vests in boats, helmets on bikes, and helmets and kneepads for inline skating.

_____ Teach your child safety rules for riding the school bus. Check with the school or bus company for a complete set of rules.

_____ Never let a child near water without an adult supervising. Teach children how to swim, but continue to supervise them directly.

_____ Teach children not to talk to strangers. Tell children that if a stranger approaches them they should run away to a safe place. Talk together about what a safe place is.

_____ Never leave children home alone.

_____ Tell children that it's never okay to fight, kick, hit, or pinch.

_____ Make sure your child has a safe way to get to school. If the route isn't safe, ride or walk to school with the child.

WORDS FOR TODDLERS

3-Letter Words	4-Letter Words	5-Letter Words	6-Letter Words
run	sing	swing	create
sit	show	paint	babble
try	jump	dance	giggle
hug	talk	slide	bounce
bow	love	watch	squirm
fly	play	laugh	tickle
ask	kiss	point	invent
eat	draw	color	splash
nap	care	smile	wiggle
hop	walk	reach	mumble
pet	leap	build	jiggle
sip	wave	share	toddle

CREATING ASSET-BUILDING MESSAGES

What you do builds assets. What you say does, too. Sometimes it's easy to get busy and not think about the words we say. In the "talk bubbles" below, write four asset-building messages that you can say to children when you see them.

QUOTES ABOUT DEVELOPMENTAL ASSETS

CHILDREN'S ASSETS

"All children need developmental assets. Every day, children need to receive continual expressions of care, guidance, and opportunities in all areas of their lives."

Nancy Leffert, Ph.D.
Coauthor, *What Young Children Need to Succeed* and
Starting Out Right: Developmental Assets for Children

"Developmental assets capture the magic and promise of childhood while equipping children with the skills they need to navigate successfully through the ups and downs of life."

Jolene L. Roehlkepartain
Coauthor, *What Young Children Need to Succeed* and
Starting Out Right: Developmental Assets for Children

SUPPORT

"Children are not properties to own and rule over, but gifts to cherish and care for. Our children are our most important guests."

Henri J. Nouwen
Professor and Author

EMPOWERMENT

"Each child deserves to be acknowledged and cherished for the qualities that maker her [or him] unique."

Lee Salk, Ph.D.
Child Development Specialist and Author

BOUNDARIES AND EXPECTATIONS

"Discipline as we see it consists of living, loving, learning; of sharing and caring; of believing and trusting; but most of all of understanding."

Louise Bates Ames, Ph.D.
Cofounder, Gesell Institute of Human Development

CONSTRUCTIVE USE OF TIME

"Art challenges children to fashion products that respond to both the inner stirrings of the soul and the outer demands of the sensory world."

Thomas Armstrong, Ph.D.
Learning Specialist and Author

QUOTES ABOUT DEVELOPMENTAL ASSETS

COMMITMENT TO LEARNING

"Children learn in every waking hour, wherever they are, whatever they are doing."

Carnegie Task Force on Learning in the Primary Grades

POSITIVE VALUES

"Children need not only food, clothing, and shelter but also purpose and principles to hold high and give direction and meaning to life."

Robert Coles, Ph.D.
Psychiatrist, Harvard University

SOCIAL COMPETENCIES

"What children need to learn is how to go about acquiring new skills to meet contemporary problems or older problems seen from a new point of view."

Margaret Mead
Anthropologist

POSITIVE IDENTITY

"Positive self-esteem comes from making the commitment to respect, accept, and love yourself completely. It's the best gift you can give yourself—and your children."

Louise Hart, Ph.D.
Psychologist and Author

YOUR FAVORITE BOOKS

Books seem to have the ability to lift us up when we're down and give us new insights when we think we've heard it all. Books can make us feel good; they can challenge us. Reading is an important asset (Asset 25) to build in children. On the books below, write the titles of four children's books that have been important to you. If you can't think of children's books, name four books that have been important to you as an adult.

If you listed children's books:

What child do you know who might enjoy one of these books? Consider giving it as a gift or checking it out of the library and reading it together.

If you listed books for adults:

Visit a library or bookstore to find something fun to read for yourself. Also find a book you'd like to share with a child.

PICTURE BOOKS THAT BUILD ASSETS

Through their stories and illustrations, picture books open up new worlds for preschoolers. Here are a few books you can share with preschoolers to build assets by reading together:

SUPPORT

Oh My Baby, Little One, written by Kathi Appelt, illustrated by Jane Dyer (New York: Harcourt, 2000). A little bird feels loved by a parent when they're together—and apart. A story that shows the wide array of ways to give love and support.

EMPOWERMENT

Mouse, Look Out! written by Judy Waite, illustrated by Norma Burgin (New York: Dutton, 1998). A mouse goes exploring, empowered by adventure. Yet the mouse also keeps an eye out for safety—from the cat. Preschoolers will delight in shouting, "Mouse, look out! There's a cat about!" as the story unfolds, and they'll love the story's fun twist at the end.

BOUNDARIES AND EXPECTATIONS

Mama, Do You Love Me? written by Barbara M. Joosse, illustrated by Barbara Lavallee (New York: Scholastic, 1992). A mother guides a daughter who is testing the limits. Preschoolers will connect with the young girl's sense of adventure as she seeks to learn just how much her mother loves her. Lush illustrations of the Inuit culture.

CONSTRUCTIVE USE OF TIME

A Mouse Told His Mother, written and illustrated by Bethany Roberts (Boston: Little, Brown and Co., 1997). A creative young mouse with a vivid imagination spends an enjoyable evening at home with his mom as he gets ready for bed.

COMMITMENT TO LEARNING

Look-Alikes Jr., written and illustrated by Joan Steiner (Boston: Little, Brown and Co., 1999). Stimulate growing minds with this picture book that has more than 700 hidden objects. Pictures include a construction site, a farm, a house, a rocket ship, and more.

POSITIVE VALUES

Farmer Duck, written by Martin Waddell, illustrated by Helen Oxenbury (Cambridge, MA: Candlewick Press, 1996). Farm animals show their care and sense of justice as they advocate for an overworked duck. This humorous book shows what happens when a committed group stands up for what's right.

SOCIAL COMPETENCIES

Click, Clack, Moo: Cows That Type, written by Doreen Cronin, illustrated by Betsy Lewin (New York: Simon & Schuster, 2000). A group of barnyard animals show how to build resistance skills (Asset 35), peaceful conflict resolution skills (Asset 36), and interpersonal skills (Asset 33) when they advocate for their needs. A humorous book that stretches preschoolers' imagination.

PICTURE BOOKS THAT BUILD ASSETS

POSITIVE IDENTITY

Amazing Grace, written by Mary Hoffman, illustrated by Caroline Binch (New York: Dial Books, 1991). Grace's grandmother believes that Grace can do anything she puts her mind to. This story illustrates just what can happen when a child dreams big and believe the best about herself (or himself).

ALL ASSETS

"More, More, More," Said the Baby, written and illustrated by Vera B. Williams (New York: Scholastic, 1991). Preschoolers will be calling for "more, more, more" when they hear this book and get caught up in the fun-loving story of three young children. The illustrations and story will encourage preschoolers to run, swing, and ask to have their belly buttons kissed. A Caldecott Honor Book.

On the Day You Were Born, written and illustrated by Debra Frasier (New York: Harcourt Brace, 1991). This classic picture book empowers children to be themselves and to know that they're loved for who they truly are. Rich illustrations accompany this uplifting story.

Time Flies, illustrated by Eric Rohmann (New York: Scholastic, 1994). Take a journey with a bird into a dinosaur museum and find out the adventures that await. One of the rare picture books that tells the story only in pictures. Preschoolers will enjoy relating the story of this Caldecott Honor Book in their own words.

I pledge to:

- **Support** children by caring about them, bringing out their best qualities, cheering them on, and celebrating who they are and what they do.

- **Empower** children by valuing them for who they are, listening to them, respecting their opinions, and helping them find ways to carry out their dreams.

- Set clear **boundaries** for children and hold children accountable when they act inappropriately, while showing them appropriate ways to act.

- **Expect** children to grow and develop, stretch their abilities, and reach their full potential.

- Advocate and ensure that children have **constructive activities**—meaningful ways to spend their time no matter where they are.

- Encourage children to have a **commitment to learning,** finding ways to make learning interesting and fun, modeling my love of learning, and tapping into the motivation that each child has within.

- Instill **positive values** in children, helping them see the importance of caring, equality, social justice, integrity, honesty, responsibility, and healthy lifestyles and sexual attitudes.

- Teach children **social competencies,** emphasizing the lifelong skills of decision making, planning, social skills, cultural competence, resistance skills, and peaceful conflict resolution.

- Help children develop a **positive identity** so that they can become who they're truly meant to be.

_____

Signature

_____

Date

THE CHILDREN YOU TOUCH

Think about one to four children who are particularly important to you—special friends, your own children, your grandchildren, your nieces and nephews, or others. Write their names in the palm of the hand.

Then think of five to ten other children whose life you touch, even in a very small way. You may see these children at work, at school, on your block, in your apartment complex, in your congregation, where you shop, through your volunteer efforts, or in other settings. Write their names in the fingers of the hand.

Keep this sheet and look at it often. Each of the children you've included on your hand represents an opportunity—and your own personal potential—for long-term asset building. As you begin to think more purposefully about asset building, you'll probably recognize that there are many other children whose lives you touch. You may want to add more names to the hand as a reminder of the many children you can support by building assets.

ADDING UP YOUR ASSET-BUILDING POTENTIAL

Asset building is powerful in two important ways. First, it's easy to do. Second, the many things you can do to build one asset often help build a number of assets at the same time. In the space below, write one simple thing you can do to build assets. Then look at the list of 40 developmental assets (see pages 16–23 in *What Young Children Need to Succeed* or Handouts #5–8). Identify which assets your action will build. For example, if you choose to smile at every child you see during the day, you'll build Asset 3: Other Adult Relationships, Asset 7: Community Values Children, Asset 14: Adult Role Models, Asset 26: Family Values Caring, and Asset 38: Self-Esteem.

My one idea to build assets in children:

This idea will build the following assets. (List one asset in each box.)

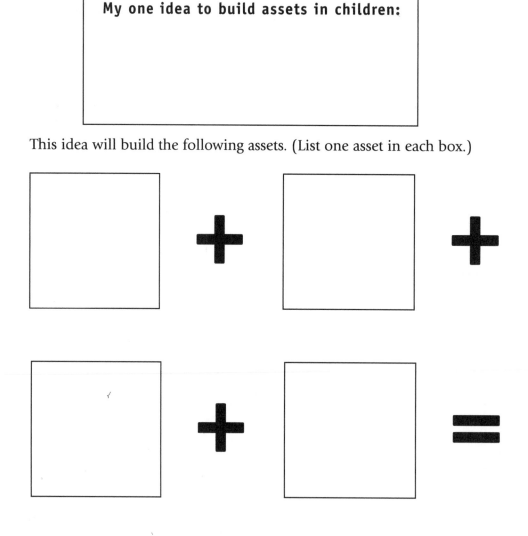

A POWERFUL ACT OF ASSET BUILDING

INDEX

Note: Locators in **bold** indicate reproducible pages.